CREATIVE Junior High PROGRAMS From A TO Z

VOL. 2 (N-Z)

*13 complete, ready-to-use
topical meetings*

If these programs work for your group, get the first half, too!

Creative Junior High Programs from A to Z, Volume 1 (A-M).

Check out www.YouthSpecialties.com for this
and other resources from Youth Specialties!

CREATIVE Junior High PROGRAMS
From A TO Z

VOL. 2 (N-Z)

*13 complete, ready-to-use
topical meetings*

Steve Dickie & Darrell Pearson

Youth Specialties

ZondervanPublishingHouse
Grand Rapids, Michigan

A Division of HarperCollinsPublishers

Creative Junior High Programs from A to Z: Vol. 2 (N-Z): 13 complete, ready-to-use topical meetings

Copyright © 1998 by Youth Specialties

Youth Specialties Books, 300 S. Pierce St., El Cajon, CA 92020, are published by Zondervan Publishing House, 5300 Patterson S.E., Grand Rapids, MI 49530.

Library of Congress Cataloging-in-Publication Data

Dickie, Steve, 1956-
      Creative junior high programs from A to Z / Steve Dickie & Darrell Pearson.
        p.   cm.
      Contents: v. 1. A-M — v. 2. N-Z.
      ISBN 0-310-20779-7 (v. 1). — ISBN 0-310-21158-1 (v. 2)
      1. Church group work with teenagers. I. Pearson, Darrell, 1954-
II. Title.
      BV4447.D479   1996
      268'.433—dc20
                                      96-20119
                                          CIP

Unless otherwise indicated, all Scripture quotations are taken from the *Holy Bible: New International Version (North American Edition).* Copyright © 1973, 1978, 1984 by International Bible Society. Used by permission of Zondervan Publishing House.

Edited by Sheri Stanley
Cover design by Patton Brothers Design
Interior design by Patton Brothers Design and Paz Design Group

Printed in the United States of America

01 02 03 04 05 06 /VG / 12 11 10 9 8 7 6 5 4 3

Darrell's dedication

To Hilary, Alyssa, and Bryn
Bright lights when my world seems dark

Steve's dedication

To Kris and Lori
Shining stars in my life

Contents

Darrell's acknowledgments

Thank you, Erlene Pearson, Erik Ewing, Chip MacEnulty, Leigh Jordan, and Megan Hughson for being wild and truthful people over the last three years.

Steve's acknowledgments

• To the junior high students and staff at Garden Grove Community Church in Garden Grove, California; South Coast Community Church in Irvine, California; Bel Air Presbyterian Church in Los Angeles, California; and Mount Hermon Christian Conference Center in Santa Cruz, California. Your lives shaped the content of this book.

• To the secretaries and administrative assistants who have been my ministry support partners over many years: Millie, Cathy, Kathy, Sharlene, Donna, Sue, Stacey, Kathy, Hayes, Teresa, Mary Ellen, Marcy, and Marilyn. Thanks for your patience, dedication, and friendship.

• To Linda Coleen Dickie, my teammate, best friend, and wife. To Wade Bass and Bobby Dickie. Thanks for allowing circus-in-my-head moments.

• To Youth Specialties and all our editors. Thanks for making ministry to students a wonderful nonboring adventure. A special thanks to Sheri Stanley and Vicki Newby for pleasant conversations and willingness to go the extra mile.

• To God. Thanks, I love you.

God's Not Boring—and Neither Are These Sessions

(or, How to Use *Creative Junior High Programs from A to Z*)

We will never forget the great insight we received from Calley, an eighth grader in one of our youth programs a number of years ago. "It's a shame," she said. "So many people think God's a drag. He's not, you know. God's not boring."

Calley was right. Very right. God's not boring. One of the greatest tragedies in the history of the church is that God is often made to seem like a drag. Don't get us wrong—the Christian faith is serious, and times of reverent respect are important. But a relationship with the Creator of the universe is far from boring.

As youth workers we have a wonderful opportunity to help junior high kids discover the passionate, thrilling, wondrous adventure called the Christian life. Sure it's tough, challenging, and sometimes scary, but in no way is it ever boring. At least it's not supposed to be. And that's where we'd like to help.

Our prayer is that you'll take advantage of your position in youth ministry to introduce junior highers to a passionate relationship with Jesus Christ. To help you in your task, we've designed twenty-six programs (13 in this book, and 13 in *Creative Junior High Programs from A-Z, Vol. 1*) that communicate life themes in creative, exciting ways. With its alphabetic sequence, the programs are each junior high-sensitive and crammed full of activities, Bible studies, illustrations, and creative alternatives designed to help kids discover our nonboring God.

Try these approaches to the meetings in this book:

Create a yearlong series.

Use these programs during a year (September through May) as weekly meeting topics. We've tried it, and it's been a big success. Start with A in September or October and finish up with Z in May or June. This plan gives you opportunities to build in some inbetween meetings to do something apart from the series, and even a month to insert a three- or four-week subtheme (like a love, sex, and dating series in February).

Darrell: A yearlong plan gives you something to promote to the parents and kids.

Steve: And it will even make you look organized to your pastor. Naturally, needs change midyear. If you need to change your original schedule, never hesitate to adjust your focus—you can always manipulate a topic title to fit your message.

Darrell: For example, once I—

Steve: I wasn't finished, Darrel.

Darrell: I take it you have more to say?

Steve: The week my group was going to do the letter M and talk about Controlling Our Mouths, the big earthquake of 1995 hit Los Angeles and creamed my church and many of our homes (including mine). That week I gathered all the students and switched the topic to a discussion on Manic Mountain Moving Motion. That's one lesson they all still remember.

 ## Let each letter stand on it's own.

Don't like the alphabetical approach? Fine. Teach the sessions in any order you like. Or teach just the sessions you like. In any case, you'll find that each session is very different from the others. We really tried to vary our approach.

Steve: I wrote the good sessions.

Darrell: Yeah, right. Don't be a dork. Okay, they're all good. Just keep the kids guessing on what's coming next. They'll love you for your creativity.

 ## Build things around the letters.

You can do all sorts of creative things for each letter. Try making a huge floor-to-ceiling letter to hang on your wall. (Try this for all twenty-six letters.) Create a couple of trivia questions that correspond to the week's letter, or give away an off-the-wall prize that begins with the letter of the week (for example, Personal Pan Pizza for P, rock for R, Vicks Vapo-Rub for V—you get the idea).

Here's a weird contest you can do each week. It's called **Can You Throw It?** Pick out an unusual object that begins with the same letter as your topic and invite several kids from your group to try to throw the object for distance. For example, cheeseburger for C, hula hoop for H, milk carton for M (empty one, please), or a seventh grader for S. Just kidding.

Steve: The more off-the-wall the better. You'll find the kids looking forward to your meeting to see what they'll be throwing.

Darrell: Weird, but fun.

 ## Use each of these programs to its best effect by—

 ## Establishing the Big Idea.

The Big Idea rises from a couple questions you need to ask yourself: What is the need of your group, and how can you meet that need? Then establish a goal—which is the Big Idea, the one thing you want your group to grasp through your program. Build your entire program around the purpose of helping your students catch the Big Idea.

Steve: Take extraordinary pains in order to create, institute, and establish this goal, which—considering the complexity of Scripture and its function as a paradigmatic template for human behavi—

Darrell: What he means is this: if you can't articulate your Big Idea simply and clearly, you'll probably have trouble with your meeting.

Now just because we've laid out the Big Ideas for each program in this book, it doesn't mean that you can't tweak, adjust, or tailor the Big Ideas—or any components in the sessions themselves—to fit your group better.

 # Maintaining the flow.

If you're new at running meetings, it's wise to begin with upbeat activities and transition to calmer ones. You want each component of the meeting to set up the next. We've designed this flow into each session. Evaluate the needs of your group and create a flow of program activities that help you achieve your Big Idea.

 # Changing the order.

We've created a sense of flow in each meeting, with each program component moving smoothly into the next. We understand, however, that our sense of order might be different than yours, so don't hesitate to change things around to fit your group. We don't mind.

 # Not trying to do it all.

We've included more ideas than you could probably ever use in one meeting. We figure that it's usually better to have loads of options than be stuck with a lot of time and nothing to do. Read through each section and decide what you're going to use and what you're going to eliminate. A tip for beginners: A common mistake is to try to do too much in one session.

Steve: Try to do everything, and you'll only confuse your group.

Darrell: You want them leaving your meeting with a clear picture of your Big Idea.

 # Adding your own material.

Use our material as a springboard for your own ideas. We think we're pretty creative people, but our stuff may be pretty lame or perhaps too bizarre for you. Dump it and try something new, or improve on our ideas. Creativity is simply giving the status quo a little twist.

Steve: And if an idea bombs, just blame us. Preserve your own credibility at all costs.

Darrell: Or tell them one of the elders suggested the idea to you. After all, it worked in *her* group in 1955.

 # Planning intentionally.

Does this sound familiar? Five minutes before the meeting, you read the session for the first time and wing it. Sure, we all do it from time to time, but please, please, please don't get too used to it. Our programs are very user-friendly, but if you want them to be great, you've got to prepare. The kids eventually see through a lack of preparation and it will hurt your ministry in the long run. Take care to do a little planning and think through what you're doing. If you're not used to this sort of deliberateness, start with this list:

- **PRAY.** Ask God to give you insight regarding your direction.

- **PLAN.** Lay out an approach to achieve what you want to accomplish.

- **PREVIEW.** Examine the meeting, determine your process, then establish the meeting's Big Idea.

- **PREPARE.** Organize what you need and get ready for the meeting.

- **PARTICIPATE.** Enable maximum involvement from your group.

- **PLAY.** Determine ways to make your meeting enjoyable.

- **PROCEED.** Carry out your meeting.

- **POSTVIEW.** Evaluate the meeting. Did you accomplish your Big Idea?

- **PRAY.** Thank God. Ask for application to be carried out by your kids.

So are you ready to go? We know you'll do a great job, and we applaud your willingness to try. Junior high kids need people like you to stick up for them, pray for them, and prove to them that God's not a drag. We believe in you and hope that our project will serve your efforts. After all, God's not boring—so we don't have to be either.

Nerves

The junior higher stands in front of the class to deliver her oral report, so nervous she can hardly swallow. When she does finally open her mouth, she hears herself say things that don't sound anything like what she wanted to say.

Life requires that we learn to master our nerves—to deliver when the moment requires. This meeting discusses how it is possible to overcome the feelings we experience when the pressure is on.

Big Idea

We can overcome our nerves when we understand that we belong to God and his Holy Spirit lives in us.

Key Text • Acts 27

When it was decided that we would sail for Italy, Paul and some other prisoners were handed over to a centurion named Julius, who belonged to the Imperial Regiment. [2]We boarded a ship from Adramyttium about to sail for ports along the coast of the province of Asia, and we put out to sea. Aristarchus, a Macedonian from Thessalonica, was with us.

[3]The next day we landed at Sidon; and Julius, in kindness to Paul, allowed him to go to his friends so they might provide for his needs. [4]From there we put out to sea again and passed to the lee of Cyprus because the winds were against us. [5]When we had sailed across the open sea off the coast of Cilicia and Pamphylia, we landed at Myra in Lycia. [6]There the centurion found an Alexandrian ship sailing for Italy and put us on board. [7]We made slow headway for many days and had difficulty arriving off Cnidus. When the wind did not allow us to hold our course, we sailed to the lee of Crete, opposite Salmone. [8]We moved along the coast with difficulty and came to a place called Fair Havens, near the town of Lasea.

[9]Much time had been lost, and sailing had already become dangerous because by now it was after the Fast. So Paul warned them, [10]"Men, I can see that our voyage is going to be disastrous and bring great loss to ship and

cargo, and to our own lives also." ¹¹But the centurion, instead of listening to what Paul said, followed the advice of the pilot and of the owner of the ship. ¹²Since the harbor was unsuitable to winter in, the majority decided that we should sail on, hoping to reach Phoenix and winter there. This was a harbor in Crete, facing both southwest and northwest.

¹³When a gentle south wind began to blow, they thought they had obtained what they wanted; so they weighed anchor and sailed along the shore of Crete. ¹⁴Before very long, a wind of hurricane force, called the "northeaster," swept down from the island. ¹⁵The ship was caught by the storm and could not head into the wind; so we gave way to it and were driven along. ¹⁶As we passed to the lee of a small island called Cauda, we were hardly able to make the lifeboat secure. ¹⁷When the men had hoisted it aboard, they passed ropes under the ship itself to hold it together. Fearing that they would run aground on the sandbars of Syrtis, they lowered the sea anchor and let the ship be driven along. ¹⁸We took such a violent battering from the storm that the next day they began to throw the cargo overboard. ¹⁹On the third day, they threw the ship's tackle overboard with their own hands. ²⁰When neither sun nor stars appeared for many days and the storm continued raging, we finally gave up all hope of being saved.

²¹After the men had gone a long time without food, Paul up stood before them and said: "Men, you should have taken my advice not to sail from Crete; then you would have spared yourselves this damage and loss. ²²But now I urge you to keep up your courage, because not one of you will be lost; only the ship will be destroyed. ²³Last night an angel of the God whose I am and whom I serve stood beside me ²⁴and said, 'Do not be afraid, Paul. You must stand trial before Caesar; and God has graciously given you the lives of all who sail with you.' ²⁵So keep up your courage, men, for I have faith in God that it will happen just as he told me. ²⁶Nevertheless, we must run aground on some island."

²⁷On the fourteenth night we were still being driven across the Adriatic Sea, when about midnight the sailors sensed they were approaching land. ²⁸They took soundings and found that the water was a hundred and twenty feet deep. A short time later they took soundings again and found it was ninety feet deep. ²⁹Fearing that we would be dashed against the rocks, they dropped four anchors from the stern and prayed for daylight. ³⁰In an attempt to escape from the ship, the sailors let the lifeboat down into the sea, pretending they were going to lower some anchors from the bow. ³¹Then Paul said to the centurion and the soldiers, "Unless these men stay with the ship, you cannot be saved." ³²So the soldiers cut the ropes that held the lifeboat and let it fall away.

³³Just before dawn Paul urged them all to eat. "For the last fourteen days," he said, "you have been in constant suspense and have gone without food—you haven't eaten anything. ³⁴Now I urge you to take some food. You

need it to survive. Not one of you will lose a single hair from his head." [35]After he said this, he took some bread and gave thanks to God in front of them all. Then he broke it and began to eat. [36]They were all encouraged and ate some food themselves. [37]Altogether there were 276 of us on board. [38]When they had eaten as much as they wanted, they lightened the ship by throwing the grain into the sea.

[39]When daylight came, they did not recognize the land, but they saw a bay with a sandy beach, where they decided to run the ship aground if they could. [40]Cutting loose the anchors, they left them in the sea and at the same time untied the ropes that held the rudders. Then they hoisted the foresail to the wind and made for the beach. [41]But the ship struck a sandbar and ran aground. The bow stuck fast and would not move, and the stern was broken into pieces by the pounding of the surf.

[42]The soldiers planned to kill the prisoners to prevent any of them from swimming away and escaping. [43]But the centurion wanted to spare Paul's life and kept them from carrying out their plan. He ordered those who could swim to jump overboard first and get to land. [44]The rest were to get there on planks or on pieces of the ship. In this way everyone reached land in safety.

What You'll Need for This Session

❋ TV, VCR, the video *Hoosiers* (see **Before the Meeting**, point 1), strip of newsprint, masking tape, and markers (see **Don't Have the Nerve?**, page 16, and **Pets, Problems, & Prayer**, page 18)
❋ 4-by-8-foot table and a one-dollar bill (see **Table Challenge**, page 16)
❋ Ten feet of rope, two paper hats (resembling a sailor's hat if possible—from a cafeteria or fast food restaurant, or party hats), and three pair of sunglasses (see **Spontaneous Melodrama**, page 16)
❋ Bibles (see **Scripture Safari**, page 17)
❋ Pet—preferably a dog (see **Before the Meeting**, point 3)

Before the Meeting

1. Cue the video *Hoosiers* to the final scene where the basketball team wins the state tournament.

2. Recruit 15 kids and a narrator for the **Spontaneous Melodrama** (page 16).

3. Arrange for one of your students to bring a pet (the more exotic, the better—any of your students have a pet python?) to the meeting. Keep the pet out of eyesight until it's time for **Pets, Problems, & Prayer** (page 18).

Don't Have the Nerve?

Begin this meeting with the *Hoosiers* video clip. In the last scene the star of the team comes through in the clutch—his confidence is equal to what is required. After showing the clip—

> **Ask your group:** *Have you ever been in a situation where you felt pressure to perform like the basketball player did? What happened? How did it end?*

Next, tape a piece of newsprint to the wall and ask your kids to brainstorm all the areas of their lives in which they need the nerve to perform. These could include sports, oral reports, student council, assemblies, reading Scripture in church, etc. Tell them that we all get into situations like this—but today they're going to learn how to find the nerve to stand up, be confident, and do what they have to do.

TABLE CHALLENGE

Place a standard 4-by-8-foot table in front of the group. Put a one-dollar bill on the table and tell the students that you have a simple challenge for them—if they have the nerve. Volunteers must start on the top of the table, climb over one end and underneath the table, and come back up the other end—without touching the floor or the table legs. (Ask two volunteers to anchor each end of the table.)

Encourage several students to try it (it's usually accomplished by a small female gymnast). Give the first winner the one-dollar bill.

Shipwreck! (A Spontaneous Melodrama)

Now call your volunteers up to perform this spontaneous melodrama. Students play the various parts, whether people or inanimate objects. The fun comes as the kids perform the hilarious actions (in parentheses) as instructed by the narrator.

Cast of characters:
- Narrator
- Ship (four kids)
- Anchors (two kids)
- Lifeboat (one kid)
- Surf (three kids with sunglasses)
- Apostle Paul
- Sailors (two kids)
- Cargo (one kid)
- Hurricane (one kid)

The story begins with the apostle Paul (everyone cheers) on board the Ship (Ship join hands and make a circle). Of course, on board the Ship are Sailors, Anchors, Cargo, and a Lifeboat (all step inside the circle). Okay, now we're ready for the story.

Paul and some other prisoners were put on a boat headed for Rome. When a gentle south wind began to blow (Hurricane blows quietly at first, then makes a lot of noise throughout the sketch), they thought everything was going to go fine. But instead, a hurricane wind—called a northeaster—blew down on the boat and began to drive the Ship along (Ship starts to move). The Sailors secured the Lifeboat to the Ship by passing a rope over and under the Ship (Sailors run the rope over and under the Lifeboat several times). They took such a battering from the Surf (Surf batters everybody) that the Sailors started to throw the Cargo overboard (Sailors throw Cargo out). When neither the sun nor the moon appeared for many days, they gave up all hope of being saved.

Then Paul stood up among them and said (Okay, Paul, repeat after me), "Men! You should have taken my advice and not sailed! But now I urge you to keep up your courage—not one person will be lost. Last night an angel of the God to whom I belong told me not to be afraid, though we still have to crash on some island" (everyone gives Paul applause for the great speech).

On the fourteenth day, the Sailors checked the depth of the ocean and discovered that it was getting shallow. They threw the Anchors overboard and prayed for daylight (Come on! Let's hear some prayer!). Then they threw the Lifeboat overboard, too. The next morning, the Ship ran aground on some remote island, and the Surf began pounding the Ship to pieces (Surf pounds ship to pieces). The soldiers got ready to kill the prisoners to keep them from escaping, but instead, they let everyone swim to shore. In this way, all 276 people on the Ship lived through the great shipwreck.

And that's it for our story—let's hear it for the incredible actors!

Scripture Safari

Divide the kids into small groups with an adult leader and a Bible for each group. Ask a volunteer in each group to read Acts 27:21-25 aloud and then have the kids discuss the following questions:

※ *What gave Paul his confidence?*

※ *How did Paul describe who God was? What do you think he meant by that?*

※ *Did Paul's confidence in God mean there wouldn't be any trouble ahead? Why or why not?*

※ *Have you experienced a time when you lacked the nerve to do something you had to do? What difference would it have made if you had the same understanding of God that Paul had?*

※ *Have you ever thought of what it means to be owned by God? What difference could this make in your life?*

Pets, Problems, & Prayer

Now ask your student to bring in his or her pet, and interview the student about what it's like having a pet. Particularly emphasize the care that the pet requires. (Domesticated pets, from canaries to pythons, depend on their human owners to feed and protect them.) Be sure to interview the pet to see how great it is to have a good owner. Then—

Tell your group: That's how Paul felt in his relationship with Christ. He didn't have to worry about the trouble he was in, because he knew that his owner was taking care of him. It didn't mean life was going to be easy—there still was the shipwreck, and Paul still had to go to trial in Rome—but he had the nerve to face these problems because he belonged to the God who was in control of everything. We can have that same confidence, too.

Then try this twist on group prayer. Tape a large piece of newsprint to the wall. Tell your group that you're going to mention a topic for prayer, and they can respond with a one-word prayer that they write on the newsprint. In silence, students walk to the wall, take a marker, and write down their one-word prayers. The prayer can go something like this:

Leader: God, we thank you tonight that you are—
(Students finish the prayer with their written responses: great, everywhere, loving, etc.)

Leader: We all face tough problems just as Paul did. Help us, Lord, as we have to face—
(school, family, friends, tests, etc.)

Leader: Help us, God, in the next few days to be more—
(like you, courageous, etc.)

When the newsprint is full of words, close in a final prayer, and save the newsprint for a future meeting.

Outsiders

We've all done it. We become so comfortable with our own circle of friends that we're unwilling to allow any outsiders into our sacred group. It's unfortunate because very often the people we try to exclude could contribute so much to our lives.

For some perverse developmental reason, junior highers love to exclude a new kid for no other reason than the outsider is new. This meeting helps kids open up to the idea that outsiders should be invited to come in—for the sake of the inner circle of group members as well as for the outsider.

Big Idea

People outside our circle of friends have a lot to contribute to us, if we will let them.

Key Text • Acts 9:10-19

[10] In Damascus there was a disciple named Ananias. The Lord called to him in a vision, "Ananias!"

"Yes, Lord," he answered.

[11] The Lord told him, "Go to the house of Judas on Straight Street and ask for a man from Tarsus named Saul, for he is praying. [12] In a vision he has seen a man named Ananias come and place his hands on him to restore his sight."

[13] "Lord," Ananias answered, "I have heard many reports about this man and all the harm he has done to your saints in Jerusalem. [14] And he has come here with authority from the chief priests to arrest all who call on your name."

[15] But the Lord said to Ananias, "Go! This man is my chosen instrument to carry my name before the Gentiles and their kings and before the people of Israel. [16] I will show him how much he must suffer for my name."

[17] Then Ananias went to the house and entered it. Placing his hands on Saul, he said, "Brother Saul, the Lord—Jesus, who appeared to you on the road as you were coming here—has sent me so that you may see again and be filled with the Holy Spirit." [18] Immediately, something like scales fell from Saul's eyes, and he could see again. He got up and was baptized, [19] and after taking some food, he regained his strength.

What You'll Need for This Session

❋ Masking tape (see **Before the Meeting**, point 2)
❋ Copies of **Outsiders** (page 23) and a Bible for each adult leader

And if you want to do the options...

❋ TV, VCR, and the video *Outsiders* (see **And if you want to do the options...** [below], point 3)
❋ Adult volunteer dressed according to your uncomfortable location—if it's cold, for example, he or she can be bundled up in coat, scarf, mittens, etc. If it's a hard or cramped space, the volunteer can be equipped with an armful of pads and pillows (see **In from the Cold**, page 22)

Before the Meeting

1. Scout out an uncomfortable outdoor location to use for **And You Thought Church Pews Were Hard...** (below). Find an uncomfortable site—maybe it's cold or dark outside, or the group has to sit on concrete. Wherever it is, it should be distractingly uncomfortable.

2. Find a carpeted room for the **Inside/Outside** game (see page 21). Use masking tape to mark out a circle 15 feet in diameter for a group of about 20 kids. Make it larger or smaller depending on the size of your group.

And if you want to do the options...

3. View the film *Outsiders* and cue up a clip of someone in pain because the were left out or pushed to the outside.

Introduction

And You Thought Church Pews Were Hard...

Invite your group to take a little journey with you. Take them outside to your uncomfortable spot. Don't make a big deal about it, just take the kids there.

Introduce the meeting as usual, pretend to ignore or explain away the first few complaints from kids about how lousy or uncomfortable the accommodations are—then finally give in to the discomfort and distraction and return to the room you started in. Debrief the experience: Why was everyone uncomfortable? Why was it hard to stick it out and overcome the discomfort? Why do we like it so much better inside? Conclude by rephrasing the gist of their comments: no one likes to be outside where it's uncomfortable, cold, damp, hard, whatever. We want to be inside, where it's warm and plush.

Next, go to the carpeted room you've prepared and play the following game.

INSIDE/OUTSIDE

This game starts with the entire group outside the circle you created with masking tape. For each round you'll call a different group into the circle. The goal for each person is to try and get everyone else out of the circle. This game can get physical, so set some guidelines: no pulling clothes, no ganging up, no running, and no tackling.

Here are some possible groups: male, female, by ages, birthdays, everybody at once, on your knees, adults only, no hands allowed for one round. When you've selected a group, send them into the circle and then start play. The game is over when only one person remains in the circle.

When the last round is played, have everyone sit inside the circle (if possible) and talk about the game using the following questions:

※ *How did it feel to win? How did it feel to get pushed out early?*
※ *Is the game fun after you've been pushed out?*

Wrap up the game and—

Say to your group: *It hurts to be on the outside looking in. Most of us want to be part of what's happening.*

Option

VIDEO CLIP

Show your clip from the movie *Outsiders*, then continue to illustrate the point with the following game.

WHAT GROUP ARE YOU IN?

For this game, instruct students to move to one side of the room or the other, depending on which group they identify with. As you read off the following groups, they should immediately move to the appropriate side.

※ Students who like sports or don't like sports
※ Students who like school or don't like school
※ Musicians or nonmusicians
※ Kids in single-parent homes or in two-parent homes
※ Students living with stepbrothers and sisters or not living with stepbrothers and sisters
※ Students who like the TV show (_____) and who don't like (_____)
※ People with pets and those without pets

When you've finished the game—

Tell your group: All of us belong to some groups, and not others. And sometimes we work really hard to keep people out of the groups we're in.

Next, divide your students into smaller groups with an adult leader for each group. Give each leader a copy of **Outsiders** (page 23) and have them lead their groups through a time of discussion.

MIRACLE CURE ROLE PLAY

Bring your small groups back together, and choose four student volunteers for this simple role play.

Three of the students portray doctors discussing the possible cure for a terrible disease. The fourth student portrays a doctor—but clearly an outsider—who has found the cure. As the first three doctors discuss the dilemma, the fourth doctor tries to offer the cure, but the first three won't give him or her a chance to explain it. They keep excluding the outsider by criticizing the person for not dressing like a doctor, not having the proper education to know anything, etc.

The role play makes the point that we sometimes exclude outsiders even when they have something significant to contribute.

Conclusion

In from the Cold

Ask your group: Who are you keeping outside that needs to be brought inside? Think of one person you know that might need to be brought into your group. How can you invite that person in? What might they be able to offer your group or your friends?"

Option

All of a sudden, have your adult volunteer barge in, dressed or equipped for the uncomfortable spot you had begun the meeting in—if it was cold there, the volunteer can be all bundled up in winter clothing...if the spot was simply hard and cramped, the volunteer can have a armful of pads and pillows. He or she says, "Excuse me—I'm looking for the junior high group. I was waiting outside for them in the alley (or wherever the spot was). Do you know where I can find them? It's, uh, really lonely out there."

Encourage your kids to make a big deal out of welcoming the outsider in.

Close by asking God to help you all to bring outsiders in.

OUTSIDERS

1. What groups do you consider yourself to be part of? (Give examples if needed—sports team, neighborhood, etc.)

2. How did you get into these groups? How do others get in?

3. Are there others who want to be in your group but aren't? What keeps them out?

4. What groups are you excluded from? What keeps you out of these groups?

5. How does it feel when you can't get into a group you want to be in?

6. Let's look at our little group. Who feels like they're part of this group? Who doesn't? What can we do to make it easier for people to become part of our group?

Listen as I read Acts 9:10-19. (Read the passage.)

7. Why was Ananias afraid of Paul? Would you have been?

8. What helped Ananias accept Paul?

9. What helped other people accept Paul?

10. Think about someone that you have a hard time letting into your group. How could you learn to let him or her in?

24

Prayer

As Christians we enjoy a wonderful privilege—the ability to talk with God. The one who created the stars of the sky and the grains of sand on the shore wants to have a regular dialog with us. God has given us prayer to accomplish this, and if we can encourage a lifestyle of prayer in our junior high people now, they will reap the benefits as they grow in the future.

Big Idea

We can talk to God just like a friend talks to a friend.

Key Text • Matthew 6:9-15

⁹"This, then, is how you should pray:

"'Our Father in heaven,
hallowed be your name,
¹⁰your kingdom come,
your will be done
on earth as it is in heaven.
¹¹Give us today our daily bread.
¹²Forgive us our debts,
as we also have forgiven our debtors.
¹³And lead us not into temptation,
but deliver us from the evil one.'

¹⁴For if you forgive men when they sin against you, your heavenly Father will also forgive you. ¹⁵But if you do not forgive men their sins, your Father will not forgive your sins."

What You'll Need for This Session

❋ Whiteboard and markers (see **So, Mr. President, Do You Ever Watch "The Simpsons"?**, page 26, **Talking with God**, page 27, and **What Do You Talk to God About?**, page 27)

❋ Index cards, pens, metal or ceramic bowl, lighter fluid, matches, and a water spray bottle (see **Sins up in Smoke**, page 29)

❋ Sheets of paper and pencils (see **Thank-you Letter to God**, page 29)

LEADER HINT

This meeting is different from some of the others—it's a prayer meeting. "Prayer meeting," some of your kids will moan. "Not a prayer meeting." Okay, prayer meetings usually don't rate high on the popularity meter, but we've made this an interesting one. Plan to pray at certain intervals throughout the meeting and fill the in-between times with active insights on prayer.

Before the Meeting

1. Write the names of several famous people on a whiteboard: the president of the United States; professional athletes; movie, TV, and music stars, etc. Make sure it's a pretty impressive list.

Introduction

So, Mr. President, Do You Ever Watch "The Simpsons"?

Tell the kids that they get to have a one-hour meeting with each of the people on your whiteboard list of famous people to talk about anything they want. They also get to ask any questions they want. Run down the list of names, asking the group what they'd ask if given the opportunity.

When you've finished, ask the group how likely it is that any of them will ever get to meet those people. The odds, they'll probably admit, just aren't that high.

Then tell your group: *While the odds of talking with these famous people are slim...[dramatic pause] we have the privilege of talking with the one who created every grain of sand on the shore, every star in the sky, and the entire universe ANY TIME WE WANT!*

The sad thing is, however, that we often don't take advantage of this privilege. We'd do anything to talk with the president or a famous movie star, but with God, it's a different story. During this meeting we're going to discuss some of the ins and outs of talking with God or praying.

Talking with God

Erase the whiteboard and write out this line from John Bunyun's classic Pilgrim's Progress:

IN PRAYER, IT IS BETTER TO HAVE A HEART WITHOUT WORDS, THAN WORDS WITHOUT A HEART.

Ask the group what they think the statement means, then tell them that prayer is a lot more than token words thrown up into the air. Prayer is a conversation with God, just like a friend would have with a friend.
Now read Exodus 33:11 aloud and—

Tell your group: *We can talk to God when we're standing, walking, running, or skating. We can talk with God while riding in the car, sitting in a crowded classroom, or resting on the sofa. We can talk with God at home, at school, in a crowd, or alone in our room. We can talk with God with our eyes open, our eyes closed, silently, or out loud. Even though praying on our knees, with our head bowed, eyes closed, and hands folded is a powerful way to concentrate and show reverence to our powerful God, it's not the only way we can pray.*

What Do You Talk to God About?

Now ask your group: *What do you talk about when you have a conversation with God? When you first build a friendship, the conversation might be on the surface level, but as you grow in the friendship, your level of communication grows, too. This is the same with God. Here's a little formula to help you get started on your conversations with God.*

Write the letters A, C, T, S, and I vertically on your whiteboard and ask the kids what they think the letters stand for. Let students take some guesses, then finish writing the words with the definitions.

A—ADORATION (Praise God for who he is.)
C—CONFESSION (Admit your sins to God.)
T—THANKS (Tell God what you are thankful for.)
S—SUPPLICATION (Ask God to supply for your specific needs.)
I—INTERCESSION (Intercede on behalf of other people's needs.)

Take a few minutes to explain each of these concepts clearly. For some junior highers, these are churchy words with little or no meaning. Make sure your kids understand these concepts in everyday language.

Group Prayer Time

Using the ACTSI acrostic as a guide, this section will help you direct your group through an active prayer time. Take one letter at a time—praying, then completing the activity. Keep the prayer times simple. You can pray out loud, silently, or both. You can pray as a large group or break into small groups. During times of silence (which could be much of the time with shy junior highers), you might want to verbally suggest things to pray about.

A—Adoration

Tell your group: *Adoration is an expression of praise for who God is and what he has done. Basically, we're telling him that we love him. Take some time, right now to praise God. Here are a few suggestions:*
* *Tell God that you love him.*
* *Praise God for the weather today.*
* *Praise God for a part of his creation that you noticed today.*
* *Praise God for his power and glory.*
* *Praise God for his unchanging faithfulness.*
* *Praise God for his patience with you.*
* *Praise God for his blessings.*

ACTIVE PRAISE

The Psalms, especially Psalms 146 to 150, are filled with praise to God. Read Psalm 150 aloud, phrase by phrase. As you do, have your kids stand and act out each phrase. Let them have fun with this—shouting, jumping, and generally whooping it up in praise to God.

C—Confession

Tell your group: *Sin creates a roadblock in our relationship with God. We need to confess our sin to God. He has already forgiven us on the Cross, but we need to admit our wrongs and confess them so our relationship can be right.*

Next, read 1 John 1:9 aloud. As you pray, ask your group to consider the following:
* *Is there anything hurting your relationship with God?*
* *Confess an unresolved conflict you have with a friend.*
* *Confess an unresolved conflict you have with your parents.*
* *Confess a bad attitude you've had.*

SINS UP IN SMOKE

Give each student an index card and a pen and ask them to write out sins they want to confess to God. When they've finished, have the kids drop their cards into a metal or ceramic bowl. Douse the cards in lighter fluid, and set them on fire. Explain how God sends our sins up in smoke through his forgiveness. Extinguish the cards with your water spray bottle. (And be careful with this activity!)

T—Thanks

Say to your group: God has done wonderful things for us. It is good for us to thank him.

Read 1 Chronicles 16:7-12 aloud to the group, then lead your kids in one-sentence prayers, using these prompters:

❊ *Thank God for today.*
❊ *Thank God for something he got you through this week.*
❊ *Thank God for someone important to you.*
❊ *Thank God for the kids in this group.*
❊ *Thank God for the leaders in this group.*
❊ *Thank God for his love and forgiveness.*

THANK-YOU LETTER TO GOD

Next, pass out sheets of paper (they should still have pens from the previous activity) and tell your kids that it's time to write a thank-you letter to God. Encourage them to thank him for specific things he's done for them. When your kids have finished, invite a few volunteers to read their letters aloud.

Encourage your kids to pick up a blank book at a stationary store to record their prayers diary-style. They will be amazed and encouraged when they look back and realize that God is truly faithful.

S—Supplication

Tell your group: *Supplication is one of those double-duty-million-dollar-super-stoked words. Basically, in the context of prayer, it means God supplies. It's important to remember that prayer is not just a grocery list of requests for God. However, God is interested in just about anything we have to say.*

Next, read Psalm 86:1-7 aloud to the group and lead them in one-sentence prayers using the following prompters:

❋ *Ask God for help with your needs at school.*
❋ *Ask God for help with your needs at home.*
❋ *Ask God for help with the needs of the church.*
❋ *Ask God for help with the needs in the youth group.*
❋ *Ask God for help with the needs in our community.*
❋ *Ask God for help with the needs of our country.*
❋ *Ask God for help with the needs of the world.*

Option

As you pray, have someone record what people are praying about. Tell the group that it's great to watch God answer our prayers. Bring the requests to next week's meeting and see what has happened. Explain that God not only hears our prayers, but also answers them as well. He may answer yes, no, or sometimes wait.

TEST TRAUMA

Read the following situation to the group:

Teresa has a big test tomorrow. She hasn't studied much for it, but she wants to do well, so she prays that God will help her get an A. How do you think God will answer that prayer? Why?

I—Intercession

Say to your group: *Intercession means to take someone else's need and intercede, or go before God, on his or her behalf.*

Read Colossians 1:9-14 and lead a time of prayer where your kids come up with a list of specific needs they can pray for on behalf of other people. (Caution: Help your kids understand that they need to exercise care when sharing needs of others. Prayer time is not gossip time.)

PRAYER WALK

When you've finished praying, take your group on a prayer walk through your church or facility. As you walk, stop at various places—Sunday school classrooms, pastor's office, choir room, hallways, your sanctuary, etc.—and pray for the people who use those rooms.

Option

Place a box in your meeting room. Invite people to put their personal prayer requests in the box. Organize a prayer team of kids who pray weekly for the needs in the box.

Conclusion

Circle Prayer

Bring your prayer time to a close by standing in a circle and joining hands. As you stand there, tell the group that there is power behind prayer. Encourage them that junior highers, united in a passion for God, can turn their world upside down. Conclude with the Lord's Prayer.

Option

While standing in the circle, ask each group member to think of one person who does not know the Lord. Encourage the group to pray for these people throughout the week.

A note from Steve: When I was a teen, a group of us started praying for one of our friends to become a Christian. After youth group one night, we felt an urgency to pray for Don again, so we asked God to grab his attention. The next Sunday our youth pastor announced that he had met with a young man named Don the night before (he didn't know we were praying for this same Don), and that Don had made a decision to trust Christ with his life. Our jaws dropped to the floor—our prayers had worked.

We shouldn't have been so surprised.

Encourage your young people to come before God with confidence. He wants to hear from them and is interested in anything they have to say.

Don't forget to hang in there yourself. Keep praying for your kids, and trust that God will do great things, even though you may not see immediate results. He *is* using you.

The People Who Brought You this Book...
invite you to discover MORE valuable youth ministry resources.

Youth Specialities has three decades of experience working alongside Christian youth workers of just about every denomination and youth-serving organization. We're here to help you, whether you're brand new to youth ministry or a veteran, whether you're a volunteer or a career youth pastor. Each year we serve over 100,000 youth workers worldwide through our training seminars, conventions, magazines, resource products, and internet Web site (www.YouthSpecialties.com).

For FREE information about ways YS can help your youth ministry, complete and return this card.

Are you:　☐ A paid youth worker　　　☐ A volunteer　　　　　　　S=480001

Name_____

Church/Org. _____

Address　☐ Church or ☐ Home _____

City _____State _____Zip _____

Daytime Phone Number (_____) _____

E-Mail _____

Denomination _____ Average Weekly Church Attendance _____

The People Who Brought You this Book...
invite you to discover MORE valuable youth ministry resources.

Youth Specialities has three decades of experience working alongside Christian youth workers of just about every denomination and youth-serving organization. We're here to help you, whether you're brand new to youth ministry or a veteran, whether you're a volunteer or a career youth pastor. Each year we serve over 100,000 youth workers worldwide through our training seminars, conventions, magazines, resource products, and internet Web site (www.YouthSpecialties.com).

For FREE information about ways YS can help your youth ministry, complete and return this card.

Are you:　☐ A paid youth worker　　　☐ A volunteer　　　　　　　S=480001

Name_____

Church/Org. _____

Address　☐ Church or ☐ Home _____

City _____State _____Zip _____

Daytime Phone Number (_____) _____

E-Mail _____

Denomination _____ Average Weekly Church Attendance _____

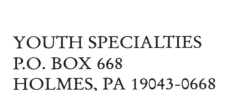

BUSINESS REPLY MAIL
FIRST-CLASS MAIL   PERMIT 268   HOLMES PA

POSTAGE WILL BE PAID BY ADDRESSEE

YOUTH SPECIALTIES
P.O. BOX 668
HOLMES, PA 19043-0668

BUSINESS REPLY MAIL
FIRST-CLASS MAIL   PERMIT 268   HOLMES PA

POSTAGE WILL BE PAID BY ADDRESSEE

YOUTH SPECIALTIES
P.O. BOX 668
HOLMES, PA 19043-0668

Quarreling

You hear it from parents all the time; the quarrels and disputes with their kids drive them crazy. Junior high students have effectively learned how to quarrel and win. Part of becoming an adult, however, means learning how to quarrel so that everyone grows through the experience. This program is designed to help kids analyze their styles of quarreling and adjust them so they become helpful rather than harmful in family relationships.

Big Idea

Quarreling isn't always bad—in fact, if it's done the right way, quarreling can be good!

Key Text • 1 Corinthians 11:1

Follow my example, as I follow the example of Christ.

What You'll Need for This Session

❋ Eight index cards and a pen (see **Before the Meeting**, point 1)
❋ TV, VCR, and video clips of sitcoms (see **Before the Meeting**, point 2)
❋ Whiteboard, markers, and Bibles (see **Microlecture**, page 35)
❋ Copies of **Bible Quarrels** (page 37) and pencils

Before the Meeting

1. On four index cards write the word PUGNACIOUS. On one of the four index cards, write the actual definition of the word, and on the other three in the set write, MAKE UP YOUR OWN CONVINCING DEFINITION.

Repeat this with four more cards and the word AFFRAY.

All these definition cards will be used for the **Dictionary Game** (page 34).

By the way, the adjective *pugnacious* describes "the condition where one is inclined to fight; a combative and argumentative person," and the verb *affray* means "to engage in perpetual fights, quarrels, brawls, or riots."

2. Record, on separate tapes, three TV sitcoms that are popular with your kids. Cue each tape to a good quarreling scene. (Don't worry—there are plenty of 'em!)

3. Arrange with an adult leader to stage a quarrel with you as the kids are arriving for the meeting. You could quarrel about who was supposed to bring refreshments, who was supposed to telephone the other, or who didn't prepare the lesson for today. Rehearse the quarrel once before the kids show up.

Introduction

Sez Who?

Start your quarrel with the other adult leader as kids arrive. Keep it off to one side as if you don't want anyone else to hear (but of course students can't *help* but hear). After several minutes, begin to take the quarrel to an absurd ending—screaming, crazy threats, whatever will make the kids realize that the whole thing is a setup. When you're done, pull the students together and—

Ask your group: *How did you feel watching us quarrel? Who seemed to be winning the argument? Why? What was each person's main goal? How well were we accomplishing our goals?*

All of us quarrel with other people from time to time. Sometimes it's at school, at home, or with friends. Today we're going to look at quarrels, and hopefully, we won't spend time quarreling about it! But first, let's play a game.

DICTIONARY GAME

In this game each contestant tries to convince the group that his or her definition of *pugnacious* and *affray* is the correct one. The catch is, one of the four definitions actually is correct (that's the definition you've already written on one of the cards).

To play, ask for four student volunteers who like weird words. Hand each of them one of the four PUGNACIOUS cards you prepared earlier. Send them out of the room to concoct a convincing but erroneous definition. When the students return, have each recite their definition in turn, and then have the audience attempt to guess which definition is correct. Reveal the true definition once the vote has been taken.

Repeat the game again by giving four different students the definition cards for AFFRAY.

34

When the game is over—

Say to your group: Our language has lots of words that have to do with fighting and quarreling. Maybe it's because we do so much of it, and there are so many ways of doing it, that it takes a lot of words to describe just how we quarrel. Anybody here want to tell us about the last rough quarrel you had?

Encourage willing students to share their quarrel stories with the group. If you have a large group, use a microphone and roam through the group. Don't critique the quarrels; simply let kids talk about their experiences. Make sure they tell how the quarrel concluded and how they felt about the experience.

When you have finished the interviews, tell them that you have some scenes from popular TV shows that feature people quarreling, and you'd like them to analyze the quarrels.

Video Clips

Show the first sitcom clip, and ask your group to analyze the quarrel. Ask questions like:
* *What was the quarrel about?*
* *Who had the upper hand? Why?*
* *Did they resolve the quarrel in the scene? Is this type of quarrel—and its resolution—likely to happen in real life?*
* *What could the characters have done to make the quarrel more fair?*
Repeat the process with the other two video clips.

Microlecture

Sketch the following diagram on your whiteboard, and tell the students that it represents how people act during quarrels.

Withdraw		Fight to win
	Resolve	
Compromise		Fight and give in

Tell your group: People react in a variety of ways when quarreling. Some people refuse to quarrel—they simply leave, head to their rooms, and slam doors behind them. This is a not a good way to quarrel—nothing ever gets resolved. Others like to fight to win the argument. They might feel pretty good about themselves, but the other person usually feels terrible. This is also not a good resolution to a quarrel. Others might fight, but eventually give in.

This isn't good either—the other person feels great, but the person who gives in always feels like a loser. Compromise seems to be a good bet, but it doesn't always work either. Both people may feel empty about what they've lost. The best way to quarrel is to work together for a resolution.

Here's how it works. Let's say you're ready to argue with your mom about your late arrival after being at the mall with your friends. You could—

* **Withdraw.** Get mad, stomp away, go to your room. Not helpful.
* **Fight to win.** Bring up times your mom has mistreated you, especially the time she knew she really blew it. The quarrel ends with her bursting into tears and leaving the room.
* **Fight and give in.** Stick up for yourself, but eventually give in because of the power of her position—hey, she's your mom! Act like everything's okay, but inside you're really angry with yourself for always giving in.
* **Compromise.** You both agree that next time, you'll come home early from the mall to make up for this time. It's a resolution, but with a price. The next time you're at the mall, you'll be embarrassed and angry when you have to leave early.
* **Resolve.** Together you hammer out a solution. Next time at the mall, you'll phone home and update her on your schedule. You and your mom both feel okay about how you resolved the quarrel.

Scripture Safari

Now divide the students into small groups, each with an adult leader. Give each group a Bible and each group member a copy of **Bible Quarrels** (page 37). Ask the students to complete the sheets and discuss the questions.

Conclusion

Pray for a Good Quarrel

Gather your whole group together again. Read 1 Corinthians 11:1 aloud then—

Say to your group: Quarrels can be hard to resolve. It's easy to fall into unhealthy patterns when we quarrel. But the Bible tells us that, with God's help, we can be like Christ in our relationships with others. God, through the Holy Spirit, can actually help us to quarrel in a godly way.

Close in group prayer. Ask your kids and adult leaders to sit in a circle and pray for the person on their right. They might pray that the next quarrel that person gets in would be handled in a godly way—the way Christ would respond. Ask God to help you all remember and apply what was discussed today when you see a quarrel evolving.

Bible Quarrels

Look up the following arguments in the Bible, and fill in your responses.

Scripture	Issue	People Involved	Resolution to Quarrel
Genesis 29:14-30			
Exodus 32:15-30			
Mark 10:41-45			

When everyone in your group has completed the boxes, discuss the following questions together:

How did each quarrel end?

Did anybody:

Withdraw? How?

Fight to win? How?

Fight and give in? How?

Compromise? How?

Resolve it? How?

Think of one tough quarrel you've had recently with somebody you care about a lot.

How did this quarrel end?

Did anybody:

Withdraw? How?

Fight to win? How?

Fight and give in? How?

Compromise? How?

Resolve it? How?

How can Jesus help you with your quarrels?

How would Jesus have acted if he was in this quarrel instead of you?

How can God help you in future quarrels?

38

Rejection

Rejection is tough to talk about with junior highers—at least it is when they're with their peers. But boy, do they experience it! Though the opening game of this session is wild and fun, the program changes quickly. This meeting is a quieter, more serious look at the pain kids experience when they are rejected by others.

Big Idea

When you're rejected, you can always find comfort in Jesus.
He knows what it feels like to be rejected.

Key Texts • Isaiah 53:3-5

³He was despised and rejected by men, a man of sorrows, and familiar with suffering. Like one from whom men hide their faces he was despised, and we esteemed him not.

⁴Surely he took up our infirmities and carried our sorrows, yet we considered him stricken by God, smitten by him, and afflicted. ⁵But he was pierced for our transgressions, he was crushed for our iniquities; the punishment that brought us peace was upon him, and by his wounds we are healed.

Luke 22:54-62

⁵⁴Then seizing him, they led him away and took him into the house of the high priest. Peter followed at a distance. ⁵⁵But when they had kindled a fire in the middle of the courtyard and had sat down together, Peter sat down with them. ⁵⁶A servant girl saw him seated there in the firelight. She looked closely at him and said, "This man was with him."

⁵⁷But he denied it. "Woman, I don't know him," he said.

⁵⁸A little later someone else saw him and said, "You also are one of them." "Man, I am not!" Peter replied.

59About an hour later another asserted, "Certainly this fellow was with him, for he is a Galilean."

60Peter replied, "Man, I don't know what you're talking about!" Just as he was speaking, the rooster crowed. 61The Lord turned and looked straight at Peter. Then Peter remembered the word the Lord had spoken to him: "Before the rooster crows today, you will disown me three times." 62And he went outside and wept bitterly.

What You'll Need for This Session

✳ At least six straw brooms, duct tape, a big soft Nerf ball, and four chairs (see **Before the Meeting**, point 1)
✳ Large piece of newsprint, tape, and broad-tip markers (see **Graffiti Wall**, page 41)
✳ A stool (see **Three Words**, page 41)
✳ Bibles (see **Talk Back**, page 42)
✳ Copies of **Missing the Cut** (page 43)

Before the Meeting

1. For **Rejection** broom hockey below, wrap the brooms with duct tape to keep the straw from falling out. For goals, set up two marker cones or chairs a few feet apart, at both ends of the playing field or room.

2. Recruit six to eight students for the drama, **Missing the Cut** (page 43). Rehearse with the Coach and the Student ahead of time.

Introduction

REJECTION

This game is a variation of broom hockey. Appoint one leader as the judge to keep score. Award a point for each *rejection* (or deflection) of a shot on goal as well as the usual point per goal. When a goal is scored or rejected the judge yells out "Goal!" or "Rejection!" As the game progresses, the judge awards two goals for each rejection.

Divide your students into two teams, then assign each team member a number—so that each team has a player 1, a player 2, etc. Line up your teams on opposite sides of the playing area, and lay the brooms down in the middle.

To start, call out any random combination of player numbers. For example, you might call out players 2, 4, and 12. The players with those numbers on each team run out, grab a broom, and try to hit the Nerf ball through the goal. Call out new numbers frequently to allow everyone the chance to play. Sometimes call out only one or two numbers to change the style of the game. Play as long as time allows.

When the game concludes, the word *rejection* will probably be on everybody's mind. Ask your group to sit down and talk about the game. What were the best rejections? Did it frustrate anyone that more points were scored for rejections than for goals? Did anyone have more fun rejecting shots than making them?

Missing the Cut

Next, introduce the drama **Missing the Cut** by telling the kids that the rejections we face everyday are not fun—they're tough. Call on your volunteers to perform the drama.

When the sketch has finished—

Tell your group: Rejection isn't easy, and often the people around us just don't understand. Rejection hurts! Let's share some examples of times we all encountered rejection with our next activity.

GRAFFITI WALL

Create a graffiti wall by taping a large strip of newsprint to one wall of your youth room. Scrawl the word REJECTION across the top, then pass out broad-tip markers to your kids. Let them walk up to the graffiti wall and write down places and events in their lives where they've experienced rejection. The newsprint will probably be fairly full when they're finished.

Discuss some of the events they've listed on the wall, asking for comments about areas of rejection that don't seem as obvious as others. Then tell the kids that you want to read a true story written by a student about a time when he put himself in a position to face either acceptance or rejection.

Three Words

Now let your group sit on the floor and get comfortable. Turn down the lights a little, and create an intimate setting for the reading of this story. Sit on a stool in the middle of the group as you read **Three Words** (page 44).

Talk Back

When you've finished the story—

Tell your group: Sad, wasn't it? Has anyone ever felt like that? Has anyone ever been rejected by someone else—not necessarily of the opposite sex, but perhaps by a parent, a teacher, or a coach? What was it like? How did it feel? How did you deal with it?
[Allow a few willing volunteers to share their experiences.] Then say: Jesus experienced rejection, too. Before he was even born, there was no room for him, and when he died, his own best friends didn't stand by him.

Now pass out Bibles and have students turn to Luke 22:54-62. After everyone has quietly read the passage, break into groups of three or four and ask the groups to discuss how Jesus must have felt at that moment. Let the discussion continue for several minutes.

Conclusion

He, Too, Was Despised and Rejected

When the discussions have finished, bring your group back together. Read Isaiah 53:3-5 aloud. Close by praying something like this—

Lord, you too were rejected by everybody around you. Thank you that you understand what it's like to be rejected. Thank you that, through your willingness to be rejected and crucified, our sins have been taken care of. Amen.

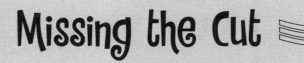

Missing the Cut

The sketch begins with four to six students crowded around an imaginary wall. They are facing the audience, who is sitting on the other side of this transparent wall. All four to six students are looking carefully and excitedly at the wall. There is a lot of discussion and arguing about who made the cut and who didn't. One by one, each student screams excitedly when he or she finds his or her name and then leaves the scene. Eventually, one student is left standing, staring blankly at the wall as he or she looks for his or her name. After a few seconds, the coach enters and stands next to the student.

Student: Uh, Coach, my name's not on the list.

Coach: Sorry, I just couldn't make room on the team for you this year.

Student: Was I really that bad?

Coach: No, you just haven't improved enough yet.

Student: So how am I supposed to improve if I can't make the team?

Coach: Ya gotta go out on your own and practice, practice, practice.

Student: That's what I did.

Coach: Well, keep working at it. You'll get it. Just remember, this experience will help you later in life. Sometimes, we're just not good enough, but I'm sure you'll overcome it. When the going gets tough, the tough get going. You'll be a better person for this, take my word for it.

(Both exit)

THREE WORDS
(used by permission of Erik Ewing)

It was warm that evening; the sun was going down behind the camp, casting long shadows across the ground. There were a few kids rushing back to the lodge, the gravel and pine needles crunching under their feet as they ran. I was sitting on top of my cabin, watching the last bit of sun disappear behind the trees.

"This is it," I said out loud to no one. At the time I thought I was talking to God, but now I think he must have been busy with a war or maybe a new star or something somewhere else. I mean, I know he can be everywhere at once, but that evening he must have been swamped.

The last bit of sun left the sky and I found myself shuddering at the sight. The sun was gone, gone until tomorrow morning when it would stick up its head and wake all the kids at camp up for another fun-filled day. But for now it was night, and again I shuddered. I stayed up on the roof until the last of the happy campers were back from their song time and evening vespers and tucked away in their bunks. I made my way down from my perch and slowly walked to her cabin, going over and over in my mind what I would say—and also making up what she would say to me.

I came to her door. She must have heard me coming because the door opened before I knocked. There she stood with the moon and a Mr. Kill bug zapper illuminating her face. She looked beautiful. It was at that moment I knew what I had to do and actually had the confidence to do it. Few words were spoken as we began a hike to the top of the hill next to the camp.

We found a nice place at the top of the hill where we could see the moon and stars clearly. This was the place I had dreamed of. Everything was going right.

"Is this okay?" she said and looked up at me with her large brown eyes.

"Yeah, this is great!" I chirped—still caught in her stare. We engaged in small talk for close to an hour. We talked about when we met, old friends, and our future plans and dreams. Here we were, two high school seniors talking like a couple of friends at a 30-year class reunion. I looked up in the sky just in time to see a shooting star. I mumbled to myself, "This is it!"

"What?" she said, as she gave me a look that made me feel really stupid.

"Oh, nothing. Well, ah, we've known each other a long time and you know you are one of my best friends. I can tell you anything and know you will listen. You are a very special part of my life."

"Thanks. I feel the same way. We have so much in common; you know, I think of you as...well, like a brother."

If you have ever been hit by a train traveling at 300 miles per hour then you can imagine the way I felt at that moment. *Brother*—that word echoed in my brain. *Brother* is the kind of word you say to someone when you're turning them down. How could she know what I was going to say? Was I that transparent?

But, being the fool I am, I couldn't let it end at that. No, I had to say it. The three words I set out to say were words I had said a thousand times to myself. After 15 minutes of shaking like I was at the North Pole, I said it, looking straight into those deep brown eyes that I had dreamed of looking into like this for the past four years. It wasn't fancy, it wasn't grand, just three simple words from a very simple guy: "I love you."

At that moment, it was as if a boulder had been lifted off my shoulders. I had said it, I'd really said it. The shaking stopped almost immediately. God could have come down from heaven in a fiery Ford wearing a T-shirt that said, "My parents went to Jerusalem and all I got was this lousy T-shirt," and I wouldn't have noticed. With the words I had said still hanging in the air, her lips parted and she took in a breath. It was like the sound of a gentle mountain stream cascading over a smooth rock. I moved closer, saying over and over in my head, "This can't be happening. This can't be happening."

And then she spoke: "Oh, wow."

I could feel blood pounding in my head, because the way she said it was the way you say "Oh wow" to a person who gave you too-small socks for Christmas. My heart jumped out and ran away, never to be seen again.

As we walked back to our cabins, I looked up into the sky and watched the stars as they twinkled down on me. If I can love the stars in their infinite space, why can't I love one girl, one five-foot-three-inch girl with brown hair and eyes to match, and with a smile that could melt any heart? I know that God has a great plan for my life, but I like to think that those plans are unfinished blueprints that he will let me help complete.

S

School

School has a major influence on junior highers' lives. Friends, peer pressure, academic tensions, athletics, self-esteem struggles, the opposite sex—they're all part of life at school. The good news is that Jesus wants to go to school right along with our junior highers. He doesn't want to live in a little box that they open only at home or at church. He wants to be part of their entire lives, even their school lives.

Big Idea

Jesus wants to be part of our lives at school.

Key Text • Proverbs 3:5-8

⁵Trust in the Lord with all your heart and lean not on your own understanding;
⁶in all your ways acknowledge him, and he will make your paths straight.
⁷Do not be wise in your own eyes; fear the Lord and shun evil.
⁸This will bring health to your body and nourishment to your bones.

This meeting is a spoof of life at school. There are more games than usual, plus some time for reflection on the importance of having Jesus become part of your students' school lives. Have fun as you plan this session, and let your imagination run wild. *There's a lot of preparation required for this meeting, so delegate much of it to volunteers or to a couple of parents—and give them at least two weeks of notice.*

What You'll Need For This Session

❋ Various items for decorating the room (see **Before the Meeting**, point 1)
❋ TV, VCR, and the *Adventures of Rocky and Bullwinkle* video (see **Before the Meeting**, point 2)
❋ Whiteboard and markers (see **Report Card**, page 50)
❋ One copy of **Schooltime Trivia** posters (pages 54-69) (see **Before the Meeting**, point 3), copies of the **Schooltime Trivia** blank answer sheet (page 53), tape, a cassette tape of fun songs or college fight songs, and a cassette player
❋ Copies of **Name That Excuse** (page 71)
❋ Your self-produced video (see **Before the Meeting**, point 4)
❋ Some school-theme prizes for the winning team—rulers, pencils (see **Final Grades**, page 52)

Before the Meeting

1. Decorate your room with a school theme. Use these ideas for starters:
❋ Cut pennants from construction paper and write on them the names of junior high/middle schools from your area. If your group is from one school, then write the names of your junior highers on the pennants. Tape the pennants around the room.
❋ On a large piece of newsprint, draw school-type scenes to cover your walls. The scenes can include lockers, hallways, groups of people, libraries, science labs, gym class, etc.
❋ Gather some athletic jerseys from your respective schools and hang them around the room.
❋ Create a fictional name for your school, then supply each leader with the initial letter (cut out of construction paper) to pin to their jackets or sweaters.
❋ Get a copy of the cartoon book, *The Lighter Side of Campus Life* (Campus Life Books, Tyndale House Publishers, Wheaton, Illinois, 1986). Photocopy a few of the cartoons, glue them to colored paper, and tape them around the room.
❋ Decorate the front of your room like a principal's office. Use a card table for a desk with a few odds and ends like a globe, books, phone, pen holder, and nameplate (fold a sheet of paper lengthwise). Set up a couple of chairs next to your desk.

2. Get a copy of the *Adventures of Rocky and Bullwinkle: Volume 8—Norman Moosewell* (Buena Vista Home Video) for **Video Clip 1** (page 50). Check with a video rental store.

3. Copy question posters (see **Schooltime Trivia**, pages 54-69). Create subject stations by taping the eight posters around the room. Cover the questions until the game begins. Copy a **Schooltime Trivia** blank answer sheet (page 53) for each team (two to four teams are suggested).

4. Choose one of the following ideas and create a video tape for **Video Clip 2** (page 51):

❋ Show up early in the morning at one of your kids' houses. Tape the student as he gets up, brushes his teeth, eats breakfast, and leaves for school.

❋ Get permission from one of your kids' schools to show up on campus and videotape that kid. Get a teacher to let you walk into her classroom and surprise her. Interview the teacher and class about that student.

❋ Arrange for a willing principal to call one of your kids to his or her office. You'll be waiting with a video camera in hand as the student walks in.

❋ Interview a few people on campus: the custodian, librarian, secretary, bus driver, crossing guard, etc.

❋ Do a video piece on the cafeteria food. Tape the food from cooking to serving.

❋ Go back and interview a former elementary school teacher about one of your kids.

5. The entire meeting is a tongue-in-cheek parody of school. The person leading the program (you?) will be the principal. Ask one of your leaders or a creative kid to be the principal's sidekick, the teacher.

Introduction

Good Morning, Students

At the start of the meeting, the teacher will ask students to take a seat and then lead the group in the following song.

SCHOOL SONG

Sing the song "Twelve Days of School" (adapted from *The Greatest Skits on Earth*, by Wayne Rice and Mike Yaconelli, Youth Specialties/Zondervan). You can have the whole group sing it, or have different people act out each part. (It's sung to the tune of "The Twelve Days of Christmas.")

On the first day of school, my mommy said to me...

(First day) Do not ever sleep in class.
(Second day) Don't forget your homework.
(Third day) Don't eat crayons.
(Fourth day) Don't chew gum.
(Fifth day) Don't pick your nose.
(Sixth day) Don't hold hands.
(Seventh day) Don't throw spitballs.
(Eighth day) Don't ever belch.
(Ninth day) Don't bug the principal.
(Tenth day) Don't be a bully.
(Eleventh day) Don't bite your toenails.
(Twelfth day) Don't talk back to teachers.

Introduce the Principal

The teacher now tells the class that the principal will be meeting with the group. The principal sits at the desk as the kids sing "Good Morning to You." The principal explains to the group that the class has been chosen to take a series of tests to prove the academic excellence of their school.

Break the group into two to four (or more) teams and encourage each one to come up with a team name. Each team will play a series of games based on academic subjects. Award grades for each game: first place=A (4 points), second place=B (3 points), third place=C (2 points), fourth place=D (1 point). (Award only A and B grades if you have two teams.)

Video Clip 1

Before you begin the games, show the hilarious cartoon clip where Bullwinkle goes to Wossamotta U as star quarterback and becomes B.M.O.C. (Big Moose on Campus).

Report Card

Keep track of team scoring on a whiteboard report card. Write the name of each team on a whiteboard and award the appropriate grades by listing them below the team names. The team with the highest grade point average wins.

SCHOOLTIME TRIVIA

Supply each team with a **Schooltime Trivia** blank answer sheet (page 53) and, at the signal, have teams wander to the eight subject stations to answer the questions. Each team should have a person manage the team's answer sheet. As your group plays the game, there should be lots of energy as students run from station to station. Play some fun music during the game—perhaps some classic college fight songs.

At the end of the game, have everyone sit with their teams. Read the answers to each subject question, and have the teams correct their sheets. Give grades for each subject. For example, if only one team had all the planets in the correct order and the rest transposed two planets, then the first place team gets an A and the other teams get B's for a second place tie. If all teams do it correctly, all teams get A's. For subjects that have multiple questions, award grades by the number of correctly answered questions.

NAME THAT EXCUSE

Hand out copies of **Name That Excuse** (page 71) to each team. Ask each team to come up with three answers per question. Teams receive 5 points if they match the number 1 answer, 4 points if they match the number 2 answer, and so on. For example, if they come up with the number 1, 3, and 5 answers they get a total of 9 points.

At the end of the game, read the answers and have teams correct their sheets. Give the team with the most points an A, the second place team a B, and so on.

Video Clip 2

Next, show your creative, self-produced video to the group.

Jesus at Your Junior High

When you've finished the video, ask your kids to name the best and worst things about school. Ask them how their faith relates or does not relate to school.

Then say to your group: Imagine for a moment that Jesus comes to school with you for a month.

Ask them to discuss the following questions:
* *What would your friends think of him?*
* *What would he think of your friends?*
* *What kind of people would he hang with?*
* *How would he dress?*
* *What would he be excited about?*
* *What would he be disappointed with?*

Scripture Safari

Read and briefly discuss the following passages. Ask students how these passages apply to life at school:
* Psalm 119:1-3
* Proverbs 9:10
* Romans 12:1-2
* Proverbs 3:5-8
* Proverbs 19:20-21
* 1 Thessalonians 5:16-18

Ask your students: What are some specific ways we can let our faith affect our school life?

As your kids brainstorm, list their ideas on the whiteboard.

If you know a schoolteacher who's a Christian, invite him or her to share how he or she lives for God in the midst of school life. You can also invite a Christian high school student to share how he or she lives for God at school.

Final Grades

Encourage your kids to allow God to influence all aspects of their school lives—academic goals, popularity, peer pressure, priorities, fears, and future.

End the meeting on an upbeat note by announcing the report card scores. Give a school-theme prize to the winning team (rulers, pencil holders, binders, lunch boxes, etc.).

Invite one or two (or more) kids to carry their Bibles with the rest of their books for a day. Have them record other students' reactions and comments, and then share their experiences with the group the following week.

SCHOOLTIME TRIVIA

TEAM NAME _____

Visit each subject station and answer the questions in the spaces provided.

English
1.
2.
3.
4.

Foreign Languages
Spanish
1.
2.
3.

German
1.
2.
3.

French
1.
2.
3.

Latin
1.
2.
3.

History
1.
2.
3.
4.
5.
6.
7.

Math
1.

Geography
1.
2.
3.
4.

Spelling
1.
2.
3.
4.
5.
6.
7.
8.
9.
10.

P.E.
1.
2.
3.
4.
5.
6.
7.
8.
9.
10.

Astronomy
1.
2.
3.
4.
5.
6.
7.
8.
9.

ENGLISH

What is the problem with each sentence?

1. Just between you and I, school is a great place.

2. Their are neat people who come to our youth group.

3. Our youth pastor is a real cool guy; everyone knows it.

4. "Do you feel good?" asked Finney.

FOREIGN LANGUAGES

Translate the words into English.

Spanish

1. cumpleaños
2. más
3. perro

French

1. maison
2. rue
3. homme

German

1. schnell
2. petsig
3. strasse

Latin

1. pater
2. noster
3. culpa

HISTORY

Match the event with the correct date.

1. VJ Day
2. Leonardo da Vinci dies
3. Castro revolution in Cuba
4. St. Francis of Assisi born
5. Mayflower lands at Plymouth Rock
6. President Woodrow Wilson dies
7. Napoléon dies

a. 1181
b. 1452
c. 1620
d. 1821
e. 1924
f. 1945
g. 1959

MATH

Solve the problem.

$$6,977,677 + 211 + 6,222 + 5,667,777 + 999 + 9 + 1,237 + 7,777,777 =$$

GEOGRAPHY

Identify these states.

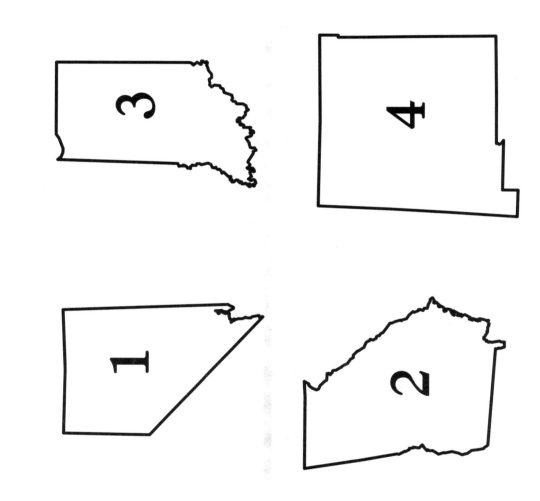

1

2

3

4

SPELLING

Which words are spelled incorrectly?

1. kalsomine
2. avoirdupoise
3. vitrescent
4. Florescent
5. creosote
6. emarginate
7. asphyxiate
8. whippoorwill
9. sublapserian
10. phenomenalism

P.E.

Name the sport played by these athletes.

1. Greg LeMond
2. Jack Nicklaus
3. Nolan Ryan
4. Joe Montana
5. Sinjin Smith
6. Wayne Gretsky
7. Larry Bird
8. Florence Joyner
9. Andre Agassi
10. Scott Hamilton

ASTRONOMY

Starting from the sun, list all nine planets in our solar system in the correct order:

SCHOOLTIME TRIVIA

Answers

English
1. you and me
2. There
3. really
4. feel well

Foreign Languages
Spanish
1. birthday
2. more
3. dog

German
1. fast
2. cutie
3. street

French
1. house
2. street
3. man

Latin
1. dad
2. our
3. fault

History
1. 1945 (f)
2. 1452 (b)
3. 1959 (g)
4. 1181 (a)
5. 1620 (c)
6. 1924 (e)
7. 1821 (d)

Math
1. 20,431,909

Geography
1. Nevada
2. Georgia
3. Indiana
4. New Mexico

Spelling
1. correct
2. avoirdupois
3. correct
4. fluorescent
5. correct
6. correct
7. correct
8. correct
9. sublapsarian
10. correct

P.E.
1. bicycle racing
2. golf
3. baseball
4. football
5. beach volleyball
6. hockey
7. basketball
8. track and field
9. tennis
10. ice skating

Astronomy
1. Mercury
2. Venus
3. Earth
4. Mars
5. Jupiter
6. Saturn
7. Uranus
8. Neptune
9. Pluto

Name That Excuse

Excuses for not having homework done
1.
2.
3.
4.
5.

Excuses for being late to class
1.
2.
3.
4.
5.

Excuses for getting a bad grade on report card
1.
2.
3.
4.
5.

Excuses given after ditching a day
1.
2.
3.
4.
5.

Excuses to get out of P.E.
1.
2.
3.
4.
5.

Name That Excuse

Excuses for not having homework done
1. I forgot.
2. I didn't know we had any homework.
3. I lost it.
4. My dog/cat/pet ate it.
5. My little brother/sister destroyed it.

Excuses for being late to class
1. I had to go to the bathroom.
2. I couldn't get my locker open.
3. My last class got out late.
4. I had to come from the other side of school.
5. I had to go to the office.

Excuses for getting a bad grade on report card
1. The teacher was unfair/bad.
2. I didn't understand the instructions.
3. The teacher didn't like me.
4. My friends kept talking to me.
5. I'm not any good at this subject.

Excuses given after ditching a day
1. I (or someone) was sick.
2. I overslept.
3. I couldn't get a ride.
4. There was a death in the family.
5. I had to watch my little brother/sister.

Excuses to get out of P.E.
1. I'm sick.
2. I'm injured.
3. I forgot my clothes.
4. I have to go to the library.
5. I'm not good at sports.

Temptation

"It seems that everything I want is either fattening, immoral, or illegal." Have you ever heard a comment like this? Sure enough, in today's world, temptation seems to come at us faster and with more complexity than ever before. The good news is that God doesn't leave us standing alone. He understands our struggles and offers us advice on how to deal with the pull to do the things we know we shouldn't do.

Big Idea

We must set up lines of defense to repel temptation.

Key Text • Romans 7:15

I do not understand what I do. For what I want to do I do not do, but what I hate I do.

What You'll Need for This Session

* Bowl of M&Ms, markers, tape, and a sheet of paper (see **Before the Meeting**, point 1)
* Large belt, large piece of cardboard, scissors or a knife, hiking boots, trash can lid, helmet, and a Bible (see **Before the Meeting**, point 2)
* Whiteboard and markers, or newsprint (see **How Can Anything That Looks This Good Be That Bad?**, page 74, **Preparing for the Attack**, page 76, **When We Are under Attack**, page 77, and **If We Give in to Temptation**, page 78)
* Extra-large pants and shirts and a few miscellaneous objects for the **Stuffed Clothes Race**, page 75
* Two large plastic garbage cans (see **Trash Can Race**, page 75)
* Spool of thread and scissors (see **Thread Snap**, page 76)
* Costume items for a military general or coach (see **Before the Meeting**, point 3)
* Three shoe boxes and an index card (see **Before the Meeting**, point 4)

Before the Meeting

1. Make a sign that says DO NOT EAT and place it over your bowl of M&Ms somewhere in the room in plain view (see **How Can Anything That Looks This Good Be That Bad?**, below).

2. Gather items to represent the armor of God (as described in Ephesians 6:14-17)—either the actual thing or a symbol for it:
   ❊ Ammo belt (truth)
   ❊ Kevlar body armor or bulletproof vest (righteousness and faith)
   ❊ Combat boots (the readiness that comes from the gospel of peace)
   ❊ Helmet (salvation)
   ❊ M-16 rifle (the Word of God)
   (see **Before we are actually tempted**, page 76).

3. Arrange for a willing student or adult with good acting skills to prepare a short pep talk. (Ideally, a military officer or even an enlisted person should do this.) Dress them appropriately—military cap, khaki, etc. Or you may wish to give this part an *athletic* rather than a *military* flavor, in which case you'd use a coach or dress a volunteer as one—cap, whistle, etc. (see **Preparing for the Attack**, page 76).

4. Write TEMPTATION on the index card, or other small piece of paper, and place it under one of the shoe boxes on a table (see **Flee Temptation Game**, page 78).

Introduction

How Can Anything That Looks This Good Be That Bad?

As your kids arrive, observe their reactions to the bowl of M&Ms and forbidding sign. When you begin your meeting, comment on the bowl. Ask how difficult it was to obey the sign. Ask your group to name some typical temptations junior highers face. Write their answers on a whiteboard or piece of newsprint.

Say to your group: Temptation is tricky. We do things we don't really want to do, and don't do things we really do want to do. As Christians, we live with this tension—we are called to righteous living, yet we struggle with temptation.

Read Romans 7:15. "I do not understand what I do. For what I want to do I do not do, but what I hate I do."

Tell your group: The apostle Paul, the ultimate example of godly living, and the same guy who wrote most of the New Testament, struggled with temptation—just as we do. And like Paul we still want to pursue a godly lifestyle.
Our challenge is faithfulness—God wants us to be faithful to his commands. Throughout Scripture, he tells us the importance of following his truths. We would be wise to follow them.

Read John 14:15. *"If you love me, you will obey what I command."*

Our struggle is temptation—Giving in to temptation is the greatest roadblock to being faithful to God's commands. If we take God seriously, we must take temptation seriously. Why do you think God is serious about temptation?

Let kids brainstorm for a while, and then offer these two reasons:

1. Temptation can prevent us from fulfilling our spiritual potential. *Temptation weighs us down and keeps us from running the race that God has set before us.*

Imagine a hundred-meter foot race in which the runners wore hockey equipment! To the contrary, runners must strip away all but the most necessary clothes so that they can run lightly and freely. In the same way, we must get rid of anything that hinders our relationship with Christ so we may run faithfully.

To illustrate this, play one or both of the following games.

STUFFED CLOTHES RACE

Ask for a couple of volunteers to compete in a race. Give each kid a pair of oversized pants (stuff the cuffs into their socks) and shirt (tuck it in the pants). Stuff all sorts of wild objects into their clothes to weigh them down. Have the kids race from one end of the room to the other.

TRASH CAN RACE

Create a few teams of three kids each. Have two teams compete by racing across the room with each team dragging a large plastic garbage can. The winner of that race competes against the next team, and so on.

2. Temptation may cause long-term problems down the road. *The consequences of giving in to temptation can plague us long after the pleasure we grabbed for has faded.*

Now illustrate this point with **Thread Snap**.

THREAD SNAP

Pull out a spool of thread and invite a strong volunteer to stand beside you. Ask the volunteer to hold two fingers together, then wrap thread around those fingers a few times. Then ask the person to break the thread apart—it should be easily done.

Next, wrap more thread around the volunteer's fingers as you tell the group that we often don't pay attention to temptation because we think it's easy to escape—later we find ourselves trapped with no way out. Keep wrapping thread as you're talking until you're sure the person won't be able to break free. Invite him or her to try. After your volunteer has given up, send him or her back with a pair of scissors.

Say to your group: A handy pair of scissors may not always be available when we need them. We must take temptation seriously and do all we can to resist its schemes. We must have a strategy.

Preparing for the Attack

Next, invite your military general or coach into the room in costume, and hold a preparing-to-battle-temptation pep rally complete with troop strategies or sports plays on a whiteboard.

When the general or coach leaves the room—

Tell your group: If we want to win the battle against temptation, we must prepare for the attack. As the soldier sits in the trenches, knowing that the enemy is nearby, he plans a strategy on how to resist the attack. In the same way, it is foolish to wait until we're attacked by temptation to figure out our battle plan. We must prepare for the attack in advance by creating three lines of defense—before we are actually tempted, when we are under attack, and what to do if we give in to temptation.

Defensive Line 1: Before we are actually tempted

Say to your group: The first thing we can do is stay away from situations that might lead to temptation.

Read 1 Thessalonians 5:22. "Avoid every kind of evil." The best way to deal with temptation is not to get into a situation that could cause us to stumble. Think ahead. What TV programs and movies should we watch? What magazines should we steer clear of? Which friends aren't good for us?
The second thing we can do is to prepare ourselves spiritually.

Read Ephesians 6:10-13. When you've finished, ask for a volunteer to come and stand beside you. Continue reading in Ephesians 6, verses 14-18. As you do, take each corresponding piece of equipment (or its facsimile) and place it on the volunteer as you describe its purpose.

* *Ammo belt—truth. Satan's lies masquerade as truth. God's truth penetrates lies.*
* *Kevlar body armor—righteousness and faith. Satan goes after our heart—our security and self-esteem. God's love for us protects our heart.*
* *Combat boots—the readiness that comes from the gospel of peace. Satan doesn't want people to hear God's message. Our willingness to tell others about Jesus gets the message out.*
* *Helmet—salvation. Head wounds can be fatal, and salvation can deflect such shots.*
* *M-16. As an offensive weapon God's Word, the Bible, can help you resist temptation.*
  God wants us to grow close to him. The closer we get to him, the further we get from things that are against God.

Encourage your kids to spend time reading the Bible, praying, and being with friends who also love God. Thank your volunteer and help remove the armor.

Defensive Line 2: When we are under attack

Now say to your group: *We will all be tempted—that's part of life. Being tempted itself is not wrong—it's when we give in to temptation that we suffer and sin.*

Write the following quote from Martin Luther on a whiteboard or piece of newsprint:

YOU CAN'T STOP A BIRD FROM FLYING OVER YOUR HEAD, BUT YOU CAN PREVENT IT FROM BUILDING A NEST THERE.

Ask your group: *How can we prevent temptation from building a nest in our hair?*

Listen to your students' input. Then present the following nest-busting strategy.

Say to your group:
1. **Ask:** *Is this temptation? People often fall in to temptation without thinking, only to regret it afterward. Asking this simple question forces us to realize what we're about to do.*
2. **Call:** *Ask God for the power to resist. The Bible tells us that God will never let us be tempted beyond our ability to resist (1 Corinthians 10:13).*
3. **Flee:** *Run away from temptation. Don't sit around and analyze the temptation—run, split, flee, go, depart, vacate the position, beat a retreat!*

Reinforce these truths with the following game.

FLEE TEMPTATION GAME

Divide the group into three teams. One person from each team goes up to the table with the three shoe boxes and stands in front of a box. On the signal, all three people look under their boxes. If they find the index card with the word TEMPTATION on it (which you secretly placed under one of the boxes), that person must run the opposite direction, tag some object you've already chosen, and return to the table. If the person can do it in a set amount of time, his or her team gets two points. If not, the team loses two points. Hide the index card under a new box and invite three different people to play. Keep a running tally on the score. Make sure to keep this game fast-paced!

When the game has finished, read Genesis 39:2-20 aloud (the story of Joseph and Potiphar's wife). Then—

Ask your group: *What did Joseph do to keep from being overtaken by temptation? What was Joseph's motivation for not giving in to temptation?*

Defensive Line 3: If we give in to temptation

Say to your group: *It will happen. Sometimes we will give in to temptation.*

Write the following saying on a whiteboard or piece of newsprint:

IT IS NOT POSSIBLE TO BE SINLESS, BUT IT IS POSSIBLE TO SIN LESS.

Then say to your group: *One of Satan's greatest tricks is to make a person who has sinned feel as if he or she is no longer worthy of God's love. Jesus went to incredible lengths to bring us back to God. He forgives us and wants us to forgive ourselves. If you have fallen to temptation, remember the Four Cs:*
Cry: *Go ahead and hurt over what you've done.*
Confess: *Face the music and tell God what you've done.*
Cleanse: *Allow God to cleanse you from your wrong.*
Carry on: *Walk in the good news of God's forgiveness.*

Conclusion

Stay Hot!

Tell your group: If we want to defeat temptation, we need the support of one another. It's vital to be active in youth group so we can enjoy that support.

Ask several people to come up, huddle tightly together, and act out the following story as you tell it.

Tell the group that your volunteers are a clump of coals in a barbecue. They keep each other white hot. Pull one person away from the group. Explain that if you pull one coal out from the other coals, that lone coal will cool. This is like the person who thinks he or she doesn't need other Christians and decides to go it alone. Place the person back into the clump. Point out that when the coal is back in the clump, the other coals will heat it up again. Conclude by telling them that we have got to keep each other hot for God in the midst of a world that wants to cool us off.

Close in silent prayer, encouraging your kids to talk to God about the temptations they may be struggling with.

This session might stir up all sorts of issues your kids are facing. Be prepared to listen and respond to these needs. You've been presented a wonderful follow-up opportunity. You may, however, not feel qualified to deal with the issues at hand. That's okay. Part of your job as a leader is to be a resource person. Byron Klaus, in his chapter in *The Complete Book of Youth Ministry* (1987, Moody Press), suggests three basic rules to consider when deciding if you need to draw on outside resources.

* **Time.** Do you have the time to take on the problem? Can you still continue to handle your other responsibilities?
* **Skill or Experience.** Do you have the capability to help in a particular situation. Do not bluff yourself or others.
* **Emotional Security.** Are you helping kids deal with problems you have never resolved in your own life? If so, you may not be able to offer legitimate help.

Need help? Ask. Start with your pastor, helping professionals in your community, and key laypeople in your church. Develop a list of resource people, so when the need arises you know who to contact. As much as possible, begin developing relationships with some of these contacts.

80

Unity

Among Christians, unity gets a lot of lip service but little action. Junior high people hear it taught and preached, then watch the adults in their world fight and disagree over the silliest things in the church. Of course, students are not any better than their adult models. They too find it tough to accept someone who is different and welcome that person as part of the body of Christ. Have you ever spent an entire retreat trying to build unity and harmony in your group, only to watch your kids argue over who sits by whom on the way home? That's what this program is all about—helping to put some action behind the concept of unity.

Big Idea

We need to accept other Christians by breaking down walls that divide us—especially other students we're excluding from our group of friends.

Key Text • Ephesians 2:13-16

¹³But now in Christ Jesus you who once were far away have been brought near through the blood of Christ.

¹⁴For he himself is our peace, who has made the two one and has destroyed the barrier, the dividing wall of hostility, ¹⁵by abolishing in his flesh the law with its commandments and regulations. His purpose was to create in himself one new man out of the two, thus making peace, ¹⁶and in this one body to reconcile both of them to God through the cross, by which he put to death their hostility.

What You'll Need for This Session

⁎ A "wall" and blankets or carpet remnants (see **Before the Meeting**, point 1)
⁎ Whiteboard and markers (see **Talk Back**, page 83)
⁎ Scrap lumber, nails, hammers, a tarp, and two pair of adult-size construction overalls (see **Before the Meeting**, point 2)
⁎ Sledgehammer (see **Let the Walls Fall Down!**, page 84)

Before the Meeting

1. Find a "wall" to use for **Wall Scramble** (below). Ideally, something five- to six-feet high that is sturdy enough to climb on and run into. Look around your church for anything that might work: sections of carpeted platform, stacks of chairs, etc. Cover the wall with blankets or carpet to make it easier to climb without getting scratched or bruised. You're basically looking for something that takes a group effort for students to climb.

2. Arrange with two adult volunteers to don the construction clothes and build a wall out of scrap wood (see **Building the Wall**, page 83). Use two-by-fours and several sheets of old plywood or building board or any scrap lumber you can find.

3. Select a student to read Ephesians 2:13-15 (page 84).

Introduction

WALL SCRAMBLE

Begin this program by breaking your group up into teams of ten. If your group is small, stay as one group. The object of this game is to see how many people a team can get over your wall in two minutes. Each team may follow any method they want to get bodies over the wall. (Ask several adults to spot the wall so no one gets hurt.) Not everybody needs to go over the wall—some students may be better at helping others over. At the end of two minutes, the next team gets a turn.

The students will discover different ways to get over the wall. Some groups might build human steps, letting a few kids climb and jump over the wall. Others will line up, and let each person climb the wall in turn. Watch students carefully to see what methods they use. Are they working together as a team? Are some students dominating the action? You'll use this information later. After the game, take a break to let students catch their breath.

Option

If you can't build a wall worth climbing over, find a large log (like the cardboard tube they roll carpet on) or a board (2-by-10 feet would do). Line up a group of kids on the log, and then ask them to rearrange themselves in different ways on the log or board—without getting off. They'll still have to work together to help each other move, but it's not as physical as **Wall Scramble.**

Talk Back

Once everyone has taken a short break—

Ask your group: *Who liked the game? Who found it frustrating? Did anyone on your team dominate? Which team did the best and why?*

Try to help the kids see that the team that worked together the best had the best score (well, it should turn out this way). The winning team usually let members do what they were best at doing; some sailing over the wall, others helping throw them over.

Next, divide your kids into groups with an adult volunteer for each group. Ask your students to talk about times they worked on projects with other students and found it difficult. Adult leaders could guide the discussion with questions such as:

❋ *Did anyone feel as if they just couldn't tolerate someone in the group?*
❋ *Was there someone who didn't carry his or her load in the preparation?*
❋ *Was there someone who was great at winging it when the presentation moment came?*

Next, ask the groups to discuss your youth group or church. Groups should discuss what makes it hard to get along with other Christians, and why it's hard to accept other's differences.

Pull out your whiteboard and markers. Call the group back together and brainstorm things that make it hard for people to get along. (Basically, students are recapping what they discussed in their small groups.) Let kids walk up to the board and write down their ideas. When they've finished, leave their ideas on the board till the end of the program.

Building the Wall

Ask students to sit in two groups, facing each other. Leave about 10 feet between the groups, and spread your tarp over the open space. Stand there for the next part of the program. This is also the place where the wall will be built.

Begin this section by paraphrasing the following mini-talk. Your attitude should be somewhat sarcastic. It will become obvious as you talk that everything you're saying is somewhat absurd. While you're talking, the two leaders dressed in construction clothes enter, carrying the construction items. Oblivious to your talk, they start constructing a wall between the two groups. When they're done, there will be a makeshift wall separating your youth.

Here's a mini-talk paraphrase—

> Getting along and accepting other Christians is tough. Let's face it. There are just some people who are hard to be around and accept. God knows that it's impossible to get along with everybody. He doesn't really expect us to accept everyone.

Some of you go to rival schools. How would it look if you were friends with someone from an inferior school? It would look foolish, of course, and God certainly doesn't want us to look foolish. No, it's better to keep away from people from different schools.

Some of you are mature eighth-graders, while some of you are only sixth-graders. Can you imagine how crazy it would be if God expected us to hang around each other? What a joke—sixth and eighth graders being friends! Some of you are remarkably cool and sophisticated, but others (the cool and sophisticated know who you are) are not very cool at all. Can you imagine how it would look to everyone if you hung out together?

Continue talking and ad-libbing about real differences among the kids in your group. The goal is to create discomfort as kids realize that God's plan is different than how they live.

Time your talk to conclude as the wall is finished (this should not take more than five minutes), and say—

Isn't it great when we don't have to work together, talk, or even see each other?

Ask the students to bow for prayer. Keep it silent for an uncomfortable length of time; then have your volunteer student read the passage from Ephesians 2:13-15 twice; once quietly, the second time more loudly.

Conclusion

Let the Walls Fall Down!

Now pray a prayer that reflects a complete change in your attitude. Ask God to forgive you for the barriers you and your group build and to help you see each other as he does. When you've finished praying, have another leader enter the room with the sledgehammer. He or she should walk slowly up to the wall, swing the hammer, and destroy it in a couple of swings leaving a pile of lumber on the floor. After applause from the group, let kids individually walk up to the whiteboard and erase the words they brainstormed earlier. During this time, have everyone sing a chorus that emphasizes unity, or play a contemporary Christian song during the activity.

Option

Try finishing with something practical and hands-on. For example, do appropriate backrubs, or have kids share with one other person their desire to show more unity in the group.

Violence

We have become an unbelievably violent society, at the root of which is a continually brooding anger. Adults and teenagers are no different. There seems to be a growing rage among young people that spills over into acts of incomprehensible anger and violence. That is our focus for this program.

Big Idea

It's a lot easier to talk about violence in society than it is to talk about the violence and anger in ourselves.

Key Text • Ephesians 4:25-27

²⁵Therefore each of you must put off falsehood and speak truthfully to his neighbor, for we are all members of one body. ²⁶"In your anger do not sin": Do not let the sun go down while you are still angry, ²⁷and do not give the devil a foothold.

What You'll Need for This Session

* Nerf balls, volleyballs, and a basketball (see **Murder Ball**, page 86)
* TV, VCR, and an action video (see **Before the Meeting**, point 1)
* Two sheets of paper or cardstock, a marker, and masking tape (see **Before the Meeting**, point 3)
* Box of long wooden matches (see **Not Angry Combustion, but Gradual Warming**, page 88)

Before the Meeting

1. Find a short clip from an action film that contains some violence. Use good judgement here and make sure it's appropriate for your group. Try to find something that will tastefully illustrate that violence saturates the media (see **Video Clip**, page 86).

2. Create a list of words or phrases for the game **Sing It Again!** or use the following: toddler songs, fast-food jingles, love, peace, joy. For the last round of the game, suggest a word like *mad* or *anger* (see **Sing It Again!**, page 87).

3. Make two signs for the **Maniacs and Mutes** talk (page 88). On one sign write MANIACS and on the other write MUTES.

Introduction

MURDER BALL

This game used to be called Dodge Ball, but now goes by the more violent name of Murder Ball (a reflection of the times). Play the game with at least two Nerf balls; don't use volleyballs as they do in gym class. The more Nerf balls you have, the more fun the game will be.

Split the group in half, and separate teams with a centerline. People on one team throw a ball and try to hit the people on the other team, without crossing the line. If they hit someone with the ball, that person goes out of the game and waits in line to get back in the game. Whenever someone catches a ball thrown by the opposing team, one player from the line can rejoin their team. The losing team is the first one to have all of their players eliminated.

Here's the twist. Near the end of the game, or when you're ready to play another round, toss in several volleyballs and a basketball. Explain that the game is too tame and you want some serious playing. As soon as kids have responded to this (some will be excited, others will be afraid), stop the game.

Ask everyone to sit down, and discuss why some kids were so excited about playing with the harder balls. Encourage several students to explain why the more violent version is more fun.

Segue by saying to your group: *That's a little bit what life in general is like these days. It seems that we all want a little more violence in our lives. Even if we don't want to be violent ourselves, we want to watch violent news stories or watch violent movies and TV shows.*

Video Clip

Show your video clip that illustrates violence.

Small Group Discussion

Now break into small groups with an adult leader for each group, and ask your groups discuss the following questions:

❋ *Why is there so much violence in movies and on TV these days?*

❋ *Do you think that the world is more violent now than it used to be? Why or why not?*

❋ *Is your school (or your friends) more violent these days? Why or why not? Is anybody trying to stop the violence?*

❋ *Have you personally experienced violent behavior? Have you been in a situation that was violent enough to scare you?*

Next, change the pace of the program by taking a break from the serious discussion and have some fun with the following game.

SING IT AGAIN!

Ask students to get into the same teams from **Murder Ball**. Each team will try to think of a popular song that uses a word or phrase that you will give them. Choose one team to go first, and give them the key word or concept. They then have 15 seconds to think of a song. When they do, someone (or the whole team) should sing a few lines. As soon as they finish, the other team plays. They have to come up with another song that uses the same word or phrase, and sing it. Play continues back and forth until one team cannot think of a song that uses the same word or phrase within 15 seconds. When that happens, the last team who sang a song wins that round, and you choose a new word or phrase.

For example, if the word *baby* was chosen, the groups might have picked songs like these:

"Baby Baby"
"Rock-a-Bye Baby"
"Baby Love"

For the final round suggest words like *mad* or *anger*. The group will struggle—it's harder to find songs to fit. When the game is over, ask your group why they found it harder to think of songs that contained words like *mad* or *anger*.

Now share a personal story about a time you became so angry you were out of control. Conclude by pointing out how we tend to focus on how violent the world around us is, but the worst violence comes from within.

Maniacs and Mutes

Explain that there are usually two types of personal responses to anger. Hold up the MANIACS sign, and talk about how some of us become maniacs when it comes to anger. We let anger consume us, and we can't control our emotions at all. Go to one side of the room and tape the sign to the wall. Next, hold up the MUTES sign, and talk about how some of us do the opposite. We become mutes, never expressing or talking about our anger. Go to the other side of the room and tape the sign to that wall.

Share the following anger-inducing examples. As you read each one, ask your kids to move to the maniac side of the room or the mute side, depending on how they would respond to each situation.

※ *You just got home from school and discovered your younger brother or sister going through your dresser drawer.*
※ *Your mom or dad has just grounded you for a week for being out with your friends too long.*
※ *A teacher wrongly accuses you of talking in class.*

Scripture Safari

Break up into smaller groups and give each group a Bible. Have the groups look up Ephesians 4:25-27.

Ask your students: *How does this passage apply to our lives? What does it say to those of us who are mutes? Maniacs?*

Possible responses: Mutes need to express anger instead of holding it inside; Maniacs need to control their anger; both need to be careful they don't sin against others.

Conclusion

Not Angry Combustion, but Gradual Warming

Take out a box of long wooden matches and strike one. As it burns, talk about the amount of heat one match provides.

Tell your group: *Placed right below your hand, it can burn you instantly. Placed above your hand, it does nothing at all. But placed next to a cold hand it can provide just enough heat to warm the hand. Anger is like that—it's not good or bad, it just has to be handled the right way. Not so intensely, that it burns others, not hidden away from problems, so it has no effect, but right alongside, so it can be expressed and not be destructive. Let's make our anger burn appropriately, to help our world will become a little less violent.*

Blow out the match and close in prayer.

Worry

A pimple on the tip of a nose, getting called on in math class, having the right kind of clothes, parents breaking up, or getting beat up after school. Worries. They come in all shapes and sizes, and they can leave us stalled and entangled in fear and apprehension, no matter what the size. Are we destined to stay stuck in the mud of worry, enslaved to the emotional ups and downs it brings? According to the creator of the universe, no way! The good news is that God says we don't have to have worries anymore—he wants to take them from us.

Big Idea

Worry keeps us from experiencing the life God intended.

Key Text • Philippians 4:4-7

⁴Rejoice in the Lord always. I will say it again: Rejoice! ⁵Let your gentleness be evident to all. The Lord is near. ⁶Do not be anxious about anything, but in everything, by prayer and petition, with thanksgiving, present your requests to God. ⁷And the peace of God, which transcends all understanding, will guard your hearts and your minds in Christ Jesus.

What You'll Need for This Session

⁂ Whiteboard and markers (see **What, Me Worry?**, page 90)
⁂ Sheets of paper and pens (see **Worry Acronym**, page 90)
⁂ Copies of **Worry Word Search** (page 97, 99), pencils, and a prize for the winner (see page 92)
⁂ Mixing bowl, spoon, vinegar, baking soda, salsa, cottage cheese, and peanut butter (see **Does Worry Cause Warts?**, page 92)
⁂ Copies of **Dear God** (page 101)
⁂ Newsprint, index cards, tape (see **Before the Meeting**, point 1)
⁂ Two marbles or wads of paper (see **Let Go of Those Worries!**, page 96)

And if you want to do the options...

❋ TV, VCR, and self-produced video of interviews (see **And if you want to do the options...** (below)

Before the Meeting

1. Draw two very large hands on a sheet of newsprint (see **Let Go of Those Worries!**, page 96).

And if you want to do the options...

2. During the week before the meeting, videotape interviews with people of various ages. Ask them to describe their worries. You can interview strangers at a shopping center, or people from your church after a Sunday morning service.

3. Invite several older teens (high school or college age) to share examples of the five pieces of advice on pages 94-96.

Introduction

What, Me Worry?

Write the following definition on your whiteboard:

A PAINFUL OR APPREHENSIVE UNEASINESS OF MIND OR BROODING FEAR ABOUT SOME CONTINGENCY.

Ask them what they think the statement defines. After a few guesses, tell them that it is the definition of *worry*—a feeling we've all experienced.

Tell your group: *Let's create our own definition of worry.*

WORRY ACRONYM

Divide the kids into smaller groups. Give each group a piece of paper and pen and ask them to write the word *worries* in bold letters, down the side of the paper. Ask each group to brainstorm a descriptive word or phrase for each letter. When they've finished, have the groups share their acronyms.

Worked up
Over
Restless
Realities
In
Everyday
Situations

Next, tell the group that the word *worry* comes from the German word *wurgen*, meaning "to choke." Explain that worry is a type of mental strangulation that cuts us off from what God desires for our lives. When we read the Bible, we discover that worry is a feeling that God never really intended us to have.

Say to your group: *We're going to explore what worry is, and discover God's point of view on worry.*

What We Worry About

Next, write the following headings on your whiteboard:

BABIES	CHILDREN	JUNIOR HIGH	SENIOR HIGH
0-5 YEARS	6-10 YEARS	11-14 YEARS	15-19 YEARS
YOUNG ADULT	MIDDLE AGE	OLDER AGE	SENIOR YEARS
20-30 YEARS	30-50 YEARS	50-65 YEARS	65+ YEARS

Ask your kids: *What are typical worries of people in each of these age groups?*

Record their ideas under the correct columns on the whiteboard.

LEADER HINT

Save the junior high column for last. After you've filled in the other groups, return to the junior high years and say, "Now let's look at the worries *we* face."

Option Video Clip

Show your video interviews on the subject of worry.

After discussing the worries of each age-group, share the following results of a national survey of teenagers naming their most serious fears (from *The Five Cries of Parents* by Merton P. and Irene A. Strommen [1985, Harper & Row]). This survey is more than a decade old, yet the results still ring true. Do these results still define your group?

❋ School performance (57%)
❋ My looks (53%)
❋ How well other kids like me (48%)
❋ That a parent might die (47%)
❋ How my friends treat me (45%)
❋ Hunger and poverty in the US (38%)
❋ Violence in the U.S. (36%)
❋ That I might lose my best friend (36%)
❋ Drugs and drinking (35%)
❋ That I might not get a good job (30%)

❋ Physical development (26%)
❋ Nuclear destruction of U.S. (25%)
❋ That my parents might divorce (25%)
❋ That I may die soon (21%)
❋ Sexual abuse (19%)
❋ That my friends will get me in trouble (18%)
❋ That I will get beat up at school (12%)
❋ Physical abuse by a parent (12%)
❋ That I might kill myself (12%)

Worry Word Search

Give each student a pencil and a copy of the **Worry Word Search** (page 97 or 99). Invite your kids to locate and circle the words that describe junior high worries. Give an appropriate prize to the student who finds the most words. (Puzzle 1 is fairly easy—vertical and horizontal, no diagonals, but some backwards. Puzzle 2 is difficult—vertical, horizontal, diagonal, and even backward diagonal. Choose the one you consider most appropriate for your group.)

WORRY CHARADES

Ask for several volunteers to come forward and pantomime typical junior high worries. See if the group can guess worries such as entering high school, trying out for an athletic team, taking a test, making their hair look right, getting a pimple on the nose, finding the right clothes, being embarrassed by parents, getting beat up at school, or going to the dentist.

Does Worry Cause Warts?

When you've finished your game of charades—

Tell your group: Worry won't cause warts, but it can cause a variety of other problems if it is left to fester.

STOMACH-ACID OBJECT LESSON

Take your mixing bowl and place it on a table. Fill the bowl with vinegar and explain to the group that the bowl represents our lives; the ingredients that we're adding represent worries. As you add different ingredients, explain that worries can cause problems in our lives. They can begin to fester and take their toll. Be sure to add baking soda to the mix. Show your students how the baking soda, vinegar, and other items bubble and curd into one gross mess.

Worry is just like this. It can cause all sorts of problems:

* **Health problems.** Statistics tell the story—one half of the hospital beds in America are filled with patients suffering from mental and nervous disorders. One out of 10 people in this country will suffer a total nervous breakdown. Ulcers (often aggravated by worry) are listed as one of the top 10 causes of death. High blood pressure, heart disease, headaches, thyroid problems, and even the common cold can be caused from stress and worry. Many doctors believe that over 80 percent of their patients could be cured if fears and worries could be reduced in their patients' lives. (Information taken from *Living Your Life as God Intended* by Jim Burns, 1985, Harvest House.)
* **Depression and fatigue.** Unprocessed worry can often lead to depression, and depression can lead to a paralyzed life. If allowed a foothold in our life, worry can control all our being and strangle out positive attitudes. Remind the group of the German word *wurgen,* meaning "to choke."
* **Missed opportunities.** As worry paralyzes us, it also keeps us from achieving goals, pursuing dreams, or taking advantage of opportunities we might have.
* **Loss of spiritual focus.** God desires our trust. When we focus on our worries, we take our eyes off God, and that's not the place to be.

Say to your group: The French word for a wooden shoe is sabot. *The word* sabotage *came into being when workers would throw their wooden shoes into the machinery to stop the work. Sabotage has now come to mean any attempt to hinder production or spoil a product. Worry is the wooden shoe that Satan wants to throw into our lives to hinder the plan of God. It paralyzes the spirit, sours our attitudes, and hinders our ability to move forward.*

How We Can Deal With Worry

Now ask your group: What advice would you offer to a friend who is worried about one of the following situations? [Ask your kids to respond to these examples:]
* *Parents getting a divorce*
* *Failing a test or class*
* *Getting a bad haircut*

* *Having your best friend move to another state*
* *Getting caught cheating on a test*
* *Dealing with the neighborhood bully*
* *Having an ill relative*

Tell the group that they can help others who are struggling with worry. The following good advice is a way to help others as well as themselves.

Option As the five pieces of good advice are shared, invite guest teens to share their stories at the appropriate times. They can offer a perspective that younger students can look up to.

Good advice #1: Put things into perspective

Tell your kids to sit back, take a deep breath, and relax for a moment.

Then ask them: *Will your worry change anything?*

The answer will probably be no. Next, read Proverbs 17:22 aloud and—

Ask your group: *What does this passage tell us about worry? How can we apply this passage to our lives?*

Allow the kids to brainstorm, and then tell the following story:

One man had his own special way of handling worry. He decided to do his worrying on one single day, Wednesday, and call it his Wednesday Worry Club. When a worry would occur during the week, he would write it down and put it into a box. On Wednesday, he would open the box and usually find that most of the things he had written down to worry about had already been settled. They just didn't seem that big anymore!

Good advice #2: Put first things first

Say to your group: *This is another way of saying "evaluate your priorities." God wants first place in our lives and he wants us to trust him in that position. When we worry about things, we are basically telling God that we don't trust him.*

Read Proverbs 3:6, 7 aloud and—

Ask your group: *What does this passage tell us about worry? How can we apply this passage to our lives?*

Allow the kids to brainstorm, then tell your group this story:

> During the German bombings of London during World War II, an old woman was asked about her extreme calm in the midst of such danger.
>
> "Well, every night I say my prayers," she said, "and I remember how the preacher tells us that God is always watching. So I go to sleep. There's no need for two of us to lie awake."

Good advice #3: Refocus our attitudes

Say to your group: *Every time a worry enters your thoughts, use it as an opportunity to thank God for something he has done for you. This mental exercise will help keep worries from taking a foothold in your life and will replace worries with peace.*

Read Philippians 4:4-7 aloud and—

Ask your group: *What does this passage tell us about worry? How can we apply this passage to our lives?*

Allow the kids to brainstorm for a few minutes.

Good advice #4: Talk to someone

Say to your group: *Christians were never supposed to go it alone. God gave us others for encouragement and support. If we fail to share our worries with others, we are skipping one of God's greatest resources in our lives. Find someone you trust, and confide your worries. Be aware that you also may need to encourage someone else with his or her worries.*

Read Galatians 6:2 aloud and—

Ask your group: *What does this passage tell us about worry? How can we apply this passage to our lives?*

Allow the kids to brainstorm for a few minutes.

Good advice #5: Give our worries to God

Say to your group: *God understands our weakness and he desires to carry our burdens for us. When you experience worry, say to God, "Lord, I want to trust you with this worry. I give it to you."*

Read 1 Peter 5:7 aloud and—

Ask your group: What does this passage tell us about worry? How can we apply this passage to our lives?

Allow the kids a few minutes to brainstorm.

Letter to God

Give each student a copy of **Dear God** (page 101). Ask them to personalize this letter by filling in the blanks. (If you prefer, write your own letter, focusing specifically on issues you've targeted for your group.)

Conclusion

Let Go of Those Worries!

When your students have finished their letters, invite two volunteers to come forward. Give each of them a marble or wad of paper. Ask them to turn and face the rest of the group. One person should extend an arm and clench his or her object tightly in a fist. The second person should extend an arm with the hand open, palm up, and object exposed. Go to the first person and—

*Say to your group: If we hold on to our worries tightly and refuse to let them go, they have to be pried from our hand. This can be difficult and painful. [**Pry open the hand finger by finger to remove the object. Then go to the second person.**] But if we open our worries to God, he can take them from us painlessly. [**Take the object out of the outstretched hand.**]*

Now take the picture of two large hands on newsprint you prepared before the meeting. Write out the words of 1 Peter 5:7 on the hands. (CAST ALL YOUR ANXIETY ON HIM, BECAUSE HE CARES FOR YOU.) Then, hand out index cards and pencils to the group. Invite them to write their worries on their cards, then tape them to the hands with an attitude of prayerful reflection.

LEADER HINT

After the meeting and with everyone gone, spend significant time praying for your kids. You might choose to symbolically destroy the cards, praying for each student as you cast their worries to the Lord.

Worry Word Search #1

Directions: Words are either horizontal or vertical (not diagonal) and may be spelled either forward or backward.

```
S A W P M T X C S D N E I R F X
D E Z A S G T E M P T A T I O N
N Z S R D R U G S N S Q R Z Z Z
E E E E H C Y M S O E E E F Y L
I C H N B Y X R S I I Z J H G G
R N T T O T W A E T L I E Z R A
F E O S D I T W N I L T C N P P
L L L T Y R E S L T U S T K H P
R O C Y O A S E L E B Y I R A E
I I C E D L T D I P M A O O I A
G V D N O U S A F M U M N W R R
A R R O R P H R M O U K Y E C A
Q L W M V O P G Y C V U S M U N
R A E F F P S R O F X D U O T C
M K S D N E I R F Y O B B H S E
O J H H H T A E D A S C H O O L
```

WORD LIST

- appearance
- body odor
- boyfriends
- bullies
- clothes
- competition
- death
- drugs
- fear
- friends
- girlfriends
- grades
- haircuts
- homework
- illness
- money
- parents
- popularity
- rejection
- school
- temptation
- tests
- violence
- war
- zits

Solutions to Worry Word Search #1

WORD LIST

- appearance
- body odor
- boyfriends
- bullies
- clothes
- competition
- death
- drugs
- fear

- friends
- girlfriends
- grades
- haircuts
- homework
- illness
- money
- parents
- popularity

- rejection
- school
- temptation
- tests
- violence
- war
- zits

Worry Word Search #2

Directions: Words may be spelled horizontally, vertically,
or diagonally—and either forward or backward.

```
W N X B B P N V S H H P V H D C
G Y U C L O T H E S I S F H S T
J C B W B P Y J J G G E Z T C Z
F D K J U U J F W U T E U O Y R
M K F Q L L Q S R A J C M E N P
N R N U L A X D C I R P C R V L
R O O G I R L F R I E N D S X O
H D I Y E I T V A T A N D A E O
P O T T S T I H I R H C D O N H
W Y C F A Y S T A O U H H S A C
I D E H T T I E M I L L N E S S
Y O J I I O P E S T N E R A P Q
R B E Z N P W M O N E Y N K U Q
F M R K A O P D E A T H P C U D
X F E A R S T S E T G R A D E S
J T E K X I D G N B X O Q C Y W
```

WORD LIST

- appearance
- body odor
- boyfriends
- bullies
- clothes
- competition
- death
- drugs
- fear
- friends
- girlfriends
- grades
- haircuts
- homework
- illness
- money
- parents
- popularity
- rejection
- school
- temptation
- tests
- violence
- war
- zits

Solutions to Worry Word Search #2

```
W N X B B P N V S H H P V H D C
G Y U C L O T H E S I S F H S T
J C B W B P Y J J G G E Z T C Z
F D K J U U J F W U T E U O Y R
M K F Q L L Q S R A J C M E N P
N R N U L A X D C I R P C R V L
R O O G I R L F R I E N D S X O
H D I Y E I T V A T A N D A E O
P O T T S I T I H I R H C D O N H
W Y C F A Y S T A O U H H S A C
I D E H T T I E M I L L N E S S
Y O J I I O P E S T N E R A P Q
R B E Z N P W M O N E Y N K U Q
F M R K A O P D E A T H P C U D
X F E A R S T S E T G R A D E S
J T E K X I D G N B X O Q C Y W
```

WORD LIST

- appearance
- body odor
- boyfriends
- bullies
- clothes
- competition
- death
- drugs
- fear

- friends
- girlfriends
- grades
- haircuts
- homework
- illness
- money
- parents
- popularity

- rejection
- school
- temptation
- tests
- violence
- war
- zits

These puzzles were created with the computer program *Ultra Find and Circle*, which is about $35 from Software Singularity, P.O. Box 2106, Greer, SC 29652-2106. A great tool for youth workers!

Dear God,

Hi, it's _____. I've learned a lot about the importance of giving my worries to you. It has made sense to me because I've been really worried about:

_____

_____

I know that you've told us in 1 Peter 5:7 to:

_____

_____

This is what I desire to do, God. I want to trust you and your plan for me instead of choosing to worry. I also give you these other worries that are in my life:

❋ _____
❋ _____
❋ _____
❋ _____

The next time I feel worry, I will put the following into practice:

_____

_____

Thank you for your love for me, God. I trust you with my life because I know that there is no better place to be.

Love,

_____

102

X

Xed out (When you don't make the grade)

X. What an intense letter! It's strong and forceful. When it's on a school paper or photo or over your name on a list, it's not a good thing. It's symbolic of being eliminated—Xed out, crossed off the list. X is used when you're just not good enough.

Big Idea

You're always good enough for God, just the way you are.

Key Texts • Mark 10:46-52

⁴⁶Then they came to Jericho. As Jesus and his disciples, together with a large crowd, were leaving the city, a blind man, Bartimaeus (that is, the Son of Timaeus), was sitting by the roadside begging. ⁴⁷When he heard that it was Jesus of Nazareth, he began to shout, "Jesus, Son of David, have mercy on me!"

⁴⁸Many rebuked him and told him to be quiet, but he shouted all the more, "Son of David, have mercy on me!"

⁴⁹"Jesus stopped and said, "Call him."

So they called the blind man, "Cheer up! On your feet! He's calling you." ⁵⁰Throwing his cloak aside, he jumped to his feet and came to Jesus.

⁵¹"What do you want me to do for you?" Jesus asked him.

The blind man said, "Rabbi, I want to see."

⁵²"Go," said Jesus, "your faith has healed you." Immediately he received his sight and followed Jesus along the road.

Psalm 142

¹I cry aloud to the Lord;
    I lift up my voice to the Lord for mercy.
²I pour out my complaint before him;
    before him I tell my trouble.

³When my spirit grows faint within me,
    it is you who know my way.
In the path where I walk
    men have hidden a snare for me.
⁴Look to my right and see;
    no one is concerned for me.
I have no refuge;
    no one cares for my life.

⁵I cry to you, O Lord;
    I say, "You are my refuge,
    my portion in the land of the living."
⁶Listen to my cry,
    for I am in desperate need;
    rescue me from those who pursue me,
    for they are too strong for me.
⁷Set me free from my prison,
    that I may praise your name.
Then the righteous will gather about me
    because of your goodness to me.

What You'll Need for This Session

❋ Bag of cheap candy (see **Excel at This Exacting Exercise**, page 105)
❋ Two long ropes (each long enough to stretch across your meeting room diagonally), blankets or sheets, and four to six volleyball-size Nerf balls (see **X Ball**, page 105)
❋ Index cards and a pen (see **Before the Meeting**, point 1)
❋ TV, VCR, and the video *The Mighty Ducks* (see **Before the Meeting**, point 2)
❋ Copies of local newspaper for each small group (see **Small Group Discussion**, page 107)

And if you want to do the options...

❋ Phosphorescent paint or a strobe light (see **And if you want to do the options...**, page 105)

Before the Meeting

1. For each round of the **Dictionary Game** (page 106) you'd like to play, use one X-word to create a set of four definition cards. See page 34 for how to play. Here is a list of X-words you can use:
❋ Xanthippe—an ill-tempered woman

- xenon—a heavy, colorless, and relatively inert gaseous element
- xeric—requiring only a small amount of moisture
- xenophobia—fear and hatred of strangers
- xylography—the art of engraving on wood

2. Find a short clip from *The Mighty Ducks* where the heroes come up short and lose (there are several toward the beginning of the video). Make sure you screen the entire clip beforehand so that nothing in the clip surprises you during the meeting itself (see **Video Clip**, page 106).

3. Ask a couple of students to share about a time when they came up short (see **Student Stories,** page 106). It should prime the pump for more sharing from others.

4. Select a student who will write a closing prayer for this meeting. The prayer should focus on thanking God for his high regard for us. Review the prayer with the student ahead of time.

And if you want to do the options...

5. Paint phosphorescent X's on the Nerf balls and play **X Ball** (below) in the dark, or rent a strobe light from a party supplies rental place.

Introduction

Excel at This Exacting Exercise

Welcome everybody by telling them it's X Night, when the letter X rules. In fact, any time someone uses a word with the letter X in it—a word that hasn't been used earlier in the night—you'll throw them a piece of candy. (If your youth budget is generous, throw dollar bills instead of candy.) If someone responds with an "Excellent!" reward them immediately with a piece of candy—then let the game begin!

X BALL

String two ropes across your room diagonally (in an X—what else?) about five or six feet off the ground. Drape sheets or blankets over the ropes, creating four distinct areas of the room. From any one section of the room, you'll have a difficult time seeing the other three sections. Break your kids into four equal groups and place a group in each area. Have the students sit on the floor; then, play volleyball with at least four Nerf balls. Anytime a ball touches the floor in a team's area, the team is penalized with a point. The object is to score the fewest points. Add more balls for more excitement.

Option

Play the game in the dark, using Nerfs with phosphorescent X's on them. A strobelight adds lots of fun, too.

DICTIONARY GAME

For directions on playing this game, see page 34. Give four volunteers the first word, and while they're out of the room working on their definitions—

Video Clip

Show *The Mighty Ducks* clip. When the scene is done, turn off the VCR and continue the—

DICTIONARY GAME: THE CONCLUSION

Bring back the four Dictionary Game contestants, and conclude the game as explained on page 34. After the correct definition is revealed, ask kids to share why they voted for the definition they did. If time permits, play more rounds of the game (using the list of words on page 104-105).

There's usually one person who draws almost no votes—ask them how it felt to have so few followers. Use this angle to segue to the next section.

Student Stories

Now ask several student volunteers to talk about a time when they came up really short—flunked a test, blew a term paper, were on the wrong end of the score when the game ended, etc. Make sure they don't just tell about the incident; get them to talk a little bit about how it felt to come up short.

SPONTANEOUS ROLEPLAY

Next, select several volunteers for spontaneous roleplays. Give them the following scenarios to act out:
* Asking for a date and being nicely told no.
* A younger sibling wanting to play in a baseball game and being told he or she isn't good enough by the older sibling.
* A child and parent discussing a bad report card.

Small Group Discussion

Now break kids into groups of three to five, with a leader in charge of each group. Give each group a copy of today's newspaper. Ask the kids to look for stories of people who haven't quite made it. They'll find stories of criminals, sports failures, defeated politicians, etc. The group leader should point out how many people are in the position of not quite succeeding. Ask the groups to discuss the following questions:

※ *In what area of your life do you feel the most like an X—like you're just not good enough? Why do you feel that way?*

※ *In what area are you most afraid of coming up short? Why?*

※ *Come up with Bible characters who came up short—who didn't quite measure up? How did they handle it?*

Next, have a volunteer in each group read the story of blind Bartimaeus from Mark 10:46-52. Then ask the groups to discuss the following questions:

※ *How did the others treat the blind man?*

※ *How do you think he felt as the crowd got on him?*

※ *How did he feel when Jesus stopped to talk to him?*

Now have the groups look at Mark 10:35-42—where the disciples are arguing about who's the greatest. Ask the groups to discuss the following question:

※ *What do you think the disciples learned from the blind man, in view of their argument right before this?*

Conclusion

Rescue Me

Bring everyone back together again for the last several minutes. Read Psalm 142 aloud and—

Say to your group: *God is there for us, no matter who we are or what we do. When we're the most down, he comes through for us. In God's eyes, all of us are always good enough to make his team.*

Look kids in the eye, then single out several students and affirm them for things that you know God really appreciates. Maybe they helped clean up after last week's program, or said hello to someone new. Find simple things to let them know that no matter who they are, God thinks they're okay.

Close by having your student author read the prayer he or she wrote beforehand.

108

Yearbook

Have you ever had one of those frustrating spring meetings where someone keeps passing a yearbook around rather than paying attention to what you're trying to accomplish? This meeting, instead of fighting the problem, works with it. Invite your students to bring their yearbooks for one of your last gatherings of the school year. Bring one of your old yearbooks—it will provide a dramatic example of the point you'll be making!

Big Idea

It's time to evaluate the year and reflect on what we've learned and how we've grown.

Key Text • Ephesians 5:15-16

¹⁵Be very careful, then, how you live—not as unwise but as wise, ¹⁶making the most of every opportunity, because the days are evil.

What You'll Need for This Session

❋ Camera with strap, loaded with film (see **Kodak Moments**, page 110)
❋ Several video cameras and lists of things to film (see **Before the Meeting**, point 1)
❋ TV, VCR, a videotape rewinder (or another VCR), self-produced **Lifestyles of the Poor and Obscure** video, a cassette of sappy background music, and a cassette player (see **Before the Meeting**, point 2)
❋ Thrift store posters and photos (see **Video Scavenger Hunt**, page 111)
❋ Junior high-age photos of your adult leaders (plus a few others of unknown adults), tape, sheets of paper, and pencils (see **Before the Meeting**, point 3)
❋ Bibles (see **Scripture Safari**, page 112)

Before the Meeting

1. If you can, get a video camera for every six to eight kids in the group. Make sure each camera has a fresh tape and a full battery. Then create a list (suggestions follow) of things for each team to film. Each list can have the same items, but they should be in a different order, so teams aren't trying to film the same event at the same time. Here's what your list may look like (feel free to add your own brainstorms):

> Your instructions are to film members of your team in the following settings. Good luck!
>
> 1. Six members of your group in a stall in a men's restroom.
> 2. Group members lying end-to-end in a stairway, stretching as many floors as you can reach.
> 3. The entire group in the smallest closet you can find.
> 4. In a nursery, imitating the normal behavior found in this room.
> 5. One member preaching a sermon from the pulpit.

2. Shoot your **Lifestyles of the Poor and Obscure** (page 111) video. Make an appointment with the parent of one of your students to film their room/home while they're at school or out of the house. Start with short segments filming your drive to the house, walking up the steps, etc. As much as possible, do a bad impression of Robin Leach. Film the student's room up-close and personal—the bathroom, clothes laying on the floor, baby pictures on the wall, etc. Do a short interview with the parents about what it's like living with their teenager (feel free to let them make stuff up!).

3. Collect old photos of your adult leaders and a few unknowns—use spouses and friends' pictures to throw a loop into the activity (see **Guess Who?**, page 111). Post the photos around the room, and underneath each picture, tape a sheet of paper for students' guesses and comments. Also, ask the adult leaders if they would be willing to share a little about their junior high years.

4. Remind your kids to bring their yearbooks to this meeting.

Introduction

Kodak Moments

Welcome the group. Explain the camera around your neck by telling them you just realized that it's going to be hard in future years to remember this youth group. You want to catch them in action during the evening so you'll have a lifelong record of your favorite group of junior highers. Sometime during this monologue, stop, stare at one of your students, and say, "Oh, that's perfect. What an expression! I want to capture that forever." Then take his or her picture, and go on with your introduction. Continue doing this periodically throughout the program.

VIDEO SCAVENGER HUNT

Break up the group into as many teams as you have video cameras. Assign an adult to each group to film the group's activities. This game is the most fun when you have the option of leaving your building and running around outside, or driving to locations in vehicles. If this is impossible, it's still fun to play right within your own building.

Give each team a camera and a list of things to film. Don't give them time to plan their shooting schedule; just give them the list and let them run. Give everyone 30 minutes to film and return to the room. Rewind the tapes and cue them while everyone watches the following video.

Video Clip

Show your **Lifestyles of the Poor and Obscure** video complete with sappy music and all.

Option

This can make a great ongoing activity. Each week film a different student's room without letting anyone know who it is. It's great fun and a good way to get students to show up—wondering if their room is next. It also gets kids to keep their rooms cleaner!

When the video ends, play each team's scavenger hunt video. Give prizes to the winning team—photos and posters you picked up at the thrift store.

GUESS WHO?

Have your kids move around the room observing the pictures of your adult leaders as junior highers. Provide pencils and ask them to write on the papers beneath each picture who they think the leader is (usually it's fairly obvious) and what they think that person was like in junior high. After several minutes, collect the photos and the comments, gather the group together, and read the comments associated with each picture.

When you're done reading each sheet and finding out who the person actually is, have a couple of leaders respond to the comments made about them. Are the student's conclusions accurate? Why or why not? What was each person really like back then? Is it fair to judge people by their pictures? Have each leader conclude with comments about how far they've come since that photo, the great things that have happened to them, etc.

Small Group Discussion

Break up into small groups for the last few minutes. Start by calling out the following words and let kids respond with the first words they think of. Don't judge them here—simply let them say what pops into their heads.

time	life	school
friends	school photo	teachers
parents	accomplishments	awards
frustrations	homework	next year

Next, have students take out their yearbooks and show their pictures, including group shots of activities, clubs, and sports they've participated in. Ask them to discuss the following questions in their groups:
* *How would you describe your year?*
* *Does your yearbook give an accurate look at your life this year? Your school? Your friends?*
* *What happened this year that is not captured in the book? What good things happened to you? What bad things?*
* *What would you do differently if you could change one thing about your past year? What will you do differently in the year ahead?*

Scripture Safari

Now pass out Bibles and turn to Ephesians 5:15-16. Ask a volunteer to read the verses aloud then—

Ask your group: *What does this passage say about time? What does it say to us about the past? The present? The future?*

Expect Extraordinary Exploits!

Bring the students back together in one group. Encourage everyone that if they've had a tough year, they still have the ability to make new choices that can improve the days ahead. If they've had a great year, remind them to be thankful for it. Conclude with an encouragement to make the most of the time they've got—to make choices that will make them proud of what happens to them next year. Close with prayer.

Zeros

We're not zeros—but, face it, we often feel like zeros. We struggle with trying to measure up to the popularity, beauty, intelligence, or abilities of others. The good news is that God doesn't look at us as zeros. He should know—he made us. He believes in us and has wonderful plans for our lives.

Big Idea

God believes in you and works in you.

Key Text • Philippians 1:6

Be confident of this, that he who began a good work in you will carry it on to completion until the day of Christ Jesus.

What You'll Need for This Session

❋ Two large plastic garbage cans and masking tape (see **Before the Meeting,** point 2)
❋ Sheets of paper, pens, and prizes (see **Paper Wad Shoot,** page 117)
❋ Nerf balls (see **Ball Shoot,** page 118)
❋ Yardstick or tape measure (see **Zeroscape,** page 118)
❋ Cassette or CD of the Degarmo and Key song "I'm Accepted" on the album *The Pledge* (Benson Records) and cassette/CD player (see **You are a big deal to God!,** page 119)
❋ Whiteboard and markers (see **We are still in process,** page 120)
❋ Three copies of **Caterpillar Flight** (page 121), three sets of cardboard butterfly wings and antennae, a deck of cards, and two stools (see **Before the Meeting,** point 4)
❋ Copies of **You're a Star!** (page 124)

Before the Meeting

1. Recruit kids for the talent show you'll hold at the start of your meeting (see **Talent Show!**, below). Have them perform in their talent areas—singing, playing a musical instrument, juggling, magic, dancing, etc.

2. Take your two large garbage and using the masking tape, place a large positive sign (+) on one and a negative sign (-) on the other (see **Sometimes We Feel Like Zeros**, below).

3. Announce the week before that kids can come dressed like their leaders for the **Look Like the Leader Contest** (page 119).

4. Recruit three students to rehearse and perform **Caterpillar Flight** (page 121) and make three sets of butterfly wings out of cardboard.

5. Fill out and sign the **You're a Star!** (page 124) certificates, one for each student in your youth group. Leave at least one signature line blank (see **You're a Star!**, page 120.)

Introduction

Talent Show!

Begin your meeting with the talent show. Don't make it a contest; there are no judges or winners. Encourage everyone that they are special and have a lot to offer the group.

Option

INCREDIBLE HUMAN TRICKS

If you can't prepare for the talent show in advance, or want to add this to the show, invite volunteers to come forward and spontaneously display an Incredible Human Trick. Many people can do outrageous things with their bodies: wiggle their ears, make odd faces, wrap legs around their head, etc. The results are usually pretty fun.

Sometimes We Feel Like Zeros

When the talent show is over—

Say to your group: *Congratulations! You are really wonderful people, loaded with gifts and talents. Many of us, however, don't always feel very gifted or talented. We often struggle with feeling like we're not worth anything at all—a zero.*

Then, ask the group (don't have them show hands) if they have ever—

❋ *pounded the sink in frustration because your hair wouldn't comb right?*
❋ *seen some of your friends make the honor roll, the basketball team, the cheer leading squad, or the band—but you didn't?*
❋ *gotten a bad grade even when you really did try hard?*
❋ *were the last one picked for teams at recess or P.E.?*
❋ *seen everyone else's parents at your game, play, or concert, but yours stayed home?*
❋ *wanted to say something to someone you liked, but were too shy to talk with them?*
❋ *had someone carelessly make a cutting remark that really hurt?*
❋ *tried to win the approval of someone important to you, but he or she just didn't seem to notice?"*

Say to your group: *Most of us have experienced some of these things and much more. At some point, we've struggled with our self-esteem and felt like a zero.*

[Pull out the two plastic garbage cans and stand between them.] *As we go through life, our self-esteem is often determined by the comments we receive from others.* **[As you talk, wad up a piece of paper and drop it into the appropriate can for each thing you share.]** *Some are positive (+) comments: encouragements, affirmations, acknowledgements, compliments, things that build us up. Some are negative (-) comments: sarcastic remarks, rejections, snubs, put-downs, things that tear us down.*

Whichever one of our cans is full often determines how we view ourselves.

Next, take a few minutes for some fun garbage can games.

Use these games to allow kids to be stars in front of the group. Many kids never get to star at anything, and games give you the opportunity to offset this with public affirmation. Search these kids out and cheer them on wildly—they'll never forget it!

PAPER WAD SHOOT

Give each student a piece of paper. Ask them to write their names on the papers, wad them up, and shoot at the trash can. Collect the wads, read the names, and give prizes to whoever made a basket.

BALL SHOOT

Divide the group into two teams. Mark off a free-throw line with masking tape and place the trash cans about 15 feet away. If you have a large group, add teams and trash cans. Line teams up at the free throw line and give them a Nerf ball (a basketball will knock the trash cans over). The teams shoot for a designated time—each kid shoots, then goes to the end of the line. Have adult volunteers retrieve the shots and count the baskets. The team that makes the most baskets wins. Encourage the teams to cheer on their shooters.

SHOWTIME

Let several volunteers perform showy dunks into the trash cans. Have the other kids cheer them on wildly. Help these kids to be stars in front of the group.

Zeroscape

When you've finished your games—

Say to your group: When you were children, your parent may have made a mark on the wall each year to measure how much taller you grew. **[Hold up your tape measure or yardstick.]** *Each year you'd compare yourself with the previous year's mark.*

Sometimes we measure ourselves against some pretty tough yardstick marks—impossibly high marks that are tough for almost anyone to meet.

Yardstick Mark 1: Beauty

Tell your group: Most people don't like the way they look. A study of American teenagers indicated that 80 percent didn't like their looks, and eight out of 10 were dissatisfied with their bodies. This isn't much of a surprise, since few of us could measure up to the people we see on TV or in magazines.

Yardstick Mark 2: Brains

Say to your group: Many people have come to the conclusion that they're dumb or stupid because they may have been laughed at, gotten a wrong answer, told they weren't very smart, or struggled with a school subject.

Yardstick Mark 3: Bucks

Now say: *Many don't feel they rate with others because they don't have the right clothes, own the right possessions, live on the right side of town, or have the right amount of money.*

When we grow up comparing ourselves to these yardstick marks, we can understand why we often feel like zeros. Few of us could measure up to these standards.

The Good News

Next—

Tell your group: *God doesn't care what the world says. He wants us to measure up to what he thinks is important. He thinks we are a pretty big deal!*

Read 1 Samuel 16:7 aloud:

> But the Lord said to Samuel, "Do not consider his appearance or his height, for I have rejected him. The Lord does not look at the things man looks at. Man looks at the outward appearance, but the Lord looks at the heart."

Now hold your **Look Like the Leader Contest** with the students who came dressed up like you or one of the leaders. Encourage them to walk like the leader, talk like the leader, and use expressions like the leader. Vote for the winning look-a-like. Then—

Say to your group: *It's healthy for people, even leaders, to laugh at themselves. It's not who we are on the outside, but who we are on the inside that matters. Why does God value the inner person more than the outward person?*

Allow a few kids to share their ideas, then present the following outline:

1. You are a big deal to God!

Ask different kids to look up and read these examples of how God feels about us:

* *John 3:16. "For God so loved the world that he gave his one and only Son, that whoever believes in him shall not perish but have eternal life."*
* *Ephesians 2:10. "For we are God's workmanship, created in Christ Jesus to do good works, which God prepared in advance for us to do."*
* *Psalm 147:10, 11. "His pleasure is not in the strength of the horse, nor his delight in the legs of man; the Lord delights in those who fear him, who put their hope in his unfailing love."*
* *Jeremiah 29:11. "For I know the plans I have for you," declares the Lord, "plans to prosper you and not to harm you, plans to give you hope and a future."*

* *1 John 3:1. "How great a love the Father has lavished on us, that we should be called children of God! And that is what we are!"*
* *Psalm 8:5. "You made him a little lower than the heavenly beings and crowned him with glory and honor."*
* *Psalm 139:14. "I praise you because I am fearfully and wonderfully made; your works are wonderful, I know that full well."*

Now play the Degarmo and Key song "I'm Accepted" from the album *The Pledge* (Benson Records).

2. We are still in process.

Next, write these letters on a whiteboard or newsprint: PBPGINFWMY.

Take suggestions from the group on what they think it means. After a few guesses, tell them it means "Please Be Patient. God Is Not Finished With Me Yet."

Say to your group: *We are still in process of becoming what God intends us to be. Even though we may not feel unique, we must remember that God is at work in us. He is molding and shaping us into a unique human being full of gifts and talents.*

Now read Philippians 1:6 aloud: "Being confident of this, that he who began a good work in you will carry it on to completion until the day of Christ Jesus."

Caterpillar Flight

Have your student volunteers perform the reader's theater **Caterpillar Flight** on page 121 (from *Super Sketches for Youth Ministry* by Debra Poling and Sharon Sherbondy, 1991 Zondervan/Youth Specialties). When they've finished the skit, have your group discuss the following questions.
* *What ridiculous, impossible, unrealistic dreams do you have that probably won't come true?*
* *What cocoons—safe, secure, nonthreatening places—do you like to stay in?*
* *What is so hard about failing? Why do so many people give up when they try something new and it doesn't work out?*
* *Why are things sometimes easier when we see that other people can do them? Why might something be harder after we find out someone else is also doing it?*
* *What is one thing that seems too good to be true about the Christian life? (see 1 Corinthians 2:9)*

Conclusion

You're a Star!

Randomly pass out the **You're a Star!** certificates (page 124) and pens, one to each student. Ask them to sign the empty line, present it to the person whose name appears as the "bearer," and say "Congratulations, God thinks you're great!" When everyone has finished, gather the group together and pray.

CATERPILLAR FLIGHT

Characters
Barry
Burt
Butterfly

Setting
Barry and Burt are sitting on stools as if in their cocoons.

Barry: *(yawns and stretches)* Good morning, Burt ol' boy. How'd you sleep?

Burt: *(snores)*

Barry: Burt! Burt! Wake up!

Burt: What are ya doin'?

Barry: Burt, it's morning. Time to wake up and greet the new day. *(sings)* Oh, what a beautiful morning!

Burt: Don't start singing! You remind me of my mother. She used to come into my room every day and say *(in a high voice)* "Rise and shine, little Burtie. Oh, what a beautiful morning." I still dread waking up.

Barry: I'm sorry Burtie, uh, I mean, Burt.

Burt: Do you know that I still have nightmares about this huge caterpillar-eating bird, who wears an apron, carries a fry pan, and sings, "Oh, what a beautiful morning," as she pushes me off my bed and out the window? I wake up in a cold sweat.

Barry: It's okay, Burt. I'll never sing again.

Burt: I'm sorry. I get carried away once in a while. I'll be fine. You know, I really like it in here. I feel so safe, so protected.

Barry: We do have nice cocoons. But I can't wait to see what happens next.

Burt: I don't want anything to happen. I'm fine just sitting here in my little cocoon being a quiet caterpillar.

Barry: How boring! Don't you want to break out of this silk ball and get some fresh air in your bones?

Burt: I don't think I have any bones. Just some flesh and guts and wiggly antennae.

Barry: Didn't you notice what someone left in our cocoons last night?

Burt: Where?

Barry: Down there!

Burt: *(Picks up two sets of cardboard wings)* Well, blow me away. What are these?

Barry: They're wings, you buffle-brained bug! Didn't your mom tell you when you were a little larva about the wing fairy?

Burt: *(doubting)* The wing fairy?

Barry: Yeah. Mom told me: *(in rhyme tone)* "When you're in your cocoon, cozy and safe, the wing fairy will come and visit your place. She will leave a gift that will let you fly, over valleys and hills and all through the sky."

Burt: That's just a fairy tale!

Barry: No, it's a fairy truth. Who else could have gotten into our cocoons?

Burt: Well, I don't believe it. And these things aren't wings. And we are caterpillars, not flies!

Barry: I know I'm not supposed to sit in here and die. We're supposed to change into something.

Burt: Impossible!

Barry: Ah ha! Directions! I knew we could find a way to get out of here.

Burt: Who put ants in your pants?

Barry: *(looking at directions)* "Step 1: Insert tab A on wing into tab B on body." Tab B on body? Hey, Burt! Do you see a tab on me anywhere?

Burt: You're going to attach those to you? What a gross out!

Barry: What's so gross about it? When you ate that baby cockroach I never screamed, "Oh, gross me out!" even though it was the grossest gross-me-out ever.

Burt: I think it's gross. Find the stupid tab yourself.

Barry: *(looks for tab B on body, trying to attach wings to body in all the wrong places, finally holding wings to head)* Does this look right, Burt?

Burt: How would I know? I've never seen a flying caterpillar!

Barry: If only I could try flying. Then I'd know if it was right. *(bounces as if trying to fly, wings still on head)* Nuts, there's no room in here. *(moves wings to stomach)* Maybe if I put them on my stomach. *(bounces in another flying attempt)* I know. If I stand on them, they'll lift me right out of this cocoon. *(moves wings to feet and attempts to fly)*

Burt: Barry, why don't you just put the wings away and forget it? *(sarcastically)* Maybe the flying instructor fairy will come tonight and teach you how to fly in your dreams.

Barry: I hate to admit it, Burt, but you're probably right. A caterpillar can't fly. This cocoon is just to curl up and die in.

Burt: But we won't die for a while. I still feel great. Wanna play cards?

Barry: I guess.

(Burt takes out cards and begins to shuffle them. Butterfly enters stage right and crosses in front of Burt and Barry. Barry sees it first.)

Barry: Burt! Burt! Look! A flying caterpillar! I knew Mom didn't lie to me! I knew this cocoon wasn't my coffin.

Burt: A flying caterpillar! That can't be! I see it, but I don't believe it.

Barry: Burt, tab B must be on my back. Please, help me.

Burt: No way, Jose. I don't want anything to do with this. It's freaky.

Barry: Burt, it's not freaky. Ya just gotta step out and go for it. *(puts wings on himself)* See, the wings fit! I'm busting out of this cell, Bucko. Are you coming?

Burt: I'm comfortable here. Besides, I don't want to be laughed at for being a sissy-looking flying caterpillar. I'm staying here.

Barry: You got your wings if you change your mind. I'll be looking for you in that big blue sky. Bye, Burt. *(breaks out of his cocoon, yelling, singing, cheering as he flies offstage)*

Burt: *(picks up wings, looks in direction Barry flew away)* Insert tab A on wings into tab B on body—gross me out!

END

YOU'RE A STAR!

Congratulations!

GOD HAS CREATED YOU WITH A WONDERFUL
AND PASSIONATE PLAN. HE BELIEVES IN YOU
AND LOVES YOU MORE THAN YOU KNOW!

I will praise you, for I am fearfully and wonderfully made.
Wonderful are your works; that I know very well. Psalm 139:14

For surely I know the plans I have for you, says the Lord, plans
for your welfare and not for harm, to give you a future with hope.
Jeremiah 29:11

Let the entire world know that the bearer of this certificate

_____

is a precious child of God and a gifted human being. God
has created this person and believes in their hopes,
dreams, and abilities.

YOU'RE A STAR! GOD'S STAR!

_____   _____   _____
Signature   Signature   Signature

RESOURCES FROM YOUTH SPECIALTIES

Youth Ministry Programming

Camps, Retreats, Missions, & Service Ideas (Ideas Library)
Compassionate Kids: Practical Ways to Involve Your Students in Mission and Service
Creative Bible Lessons from the Old Testament
Creative Bible Lessons in 1 & 2 Corinthians
Creative Bible Lessons in John: Encounters with Jesus
Creative Bible Lessons in Romans: Faith on Fire!
Creative Bible Lessons on the Life of Christ
Creative Bible Lessons in Psalms
Creative Junior High Programs from A to Z, Vol. 1 (A-M)
Creative Junior High Programs from A to Z, Vol. 2 (N-Z)
Creative Meetings, Bible Lessons, & Worship Ideas (Ideas Library)
Crowd Breakers & Mixers (Ideas Library)
Downloading the Bible Leader's Guide
Drama, Skits, & Sketches (Ideas Library)
Drama, Skits, & Sketches 2 (Ideas Library)
Dramatic Pauses
Everyday Object Lessons
Games (Ideas Library)
Games 2 (Ideas Library)
Good Sex: A Whole-Person Approach to Teenage Sexuality and God
Great Fundraising Ideas for Youth Groups
More Great Fundraising Ideas for Youth Groups
Great Retreats for Youth Groups
Holiday Ideas (Ideas Library)
Hot Illustrations for Youth Talks
More Hot Illustrations for Youth Talks
Still More Hot Illustrations for Youth Talks
Ideas Library on CD-ROM
Incredible Questionnaires for Youth Ministry
Junior High Game Nights
More Junior High Game Nights
Kickstarters: 101 Ingenious Intros to Just about Any Bible Lesson
Live the Life! Student Evangelism Training Kit
Memory Makers
The Next Level Leader's Guide
Play It! Over 150 Great Games for Youth Groups
Roaring Lambs
Special Events (Ideas Library)
Spontaneous Melodramas
Student Leadership Training Manual
Student Underground: An Event Curriculum on the Persecuted Church
Super Sketches for Youth Ministry
Talking the Walk
Teaching the Bible Creatively
Videos That Teach
What Would Jesus Do? Youth Leader's Kit
Wild Truth Bible Lessons
Wild Truth Bible Lessons 2
Wild Truth Bible Lessons—Pictures of God
Worship Services for Youth Groups

Professional Resources

Administration, Publicity, & Fundraising (Ideas Library)
Equipped to Serve: Volunteer Youth Worker Training Course
Help! I'm a Junior High Youth Worker!
Help! I'm a Small-Group Leader!
Help! I'm a Sunday School Teacher!
Help! I'm a Volunteer Youth Worker!
How to Expand Your Youth Ministry
How to Speak to Youth...and Keep Them Awake at the Same Time
Junior High Ministry (Updated & Expanded)
The Ministry of Nurture: A Youth Worker's Guide to Discipling Teenagers
Purpose-Driven Youth Ministry
Purpose-Driven Youth Ministry Training Kit
So That's Why I Keep Doing This! 52 Devotional Stories for Youth Workers
A Youth Ministry Crash Course

The Youth Worker's Handbook to Family Ministry

Discussion Starters

Discussion & Lesson Starters (Ideas Library)
Discussion & Lesson Starters 2 (Ideas Library)
EdgeTV
Get 'Em Talking
Keep 'Em Talking!
High School TalkSheets
More High School TalkSheets
High School TalkSheets: Psalms and Proverbs
Junior High TalkSheets
More Junior High TalkSheets
Junior High TalkSheets: Psalms and Proverbs
Real Kids: Short Cuts
Real Kids: The Real Deal—on Friendship, Loneliness, Racism, & Suicide
Real Kids: The Real Deal—on Sexual Choices, Family Matters, & Loss
Real Kids: The Real Deal—on Stressing Out, Addictive Behavior, Great Comebacks, & Violence
Real Kids: Word on the Street
Have You Ever...? 450 Intriguing Questions Guaranteed to Get Teenagers Talking
Unfinished Sentences: 450 Tantalizing Statement Starters to Get Teenagers Talking & Thinking
What If...? 450 Thought-Provoking Questions to Get Teenagers Talking, Laughing, and Thinking
Would You Rather...? 465 Provocative Questions to Get Teenagers Talking

Art Source Clip Art

Stark Raving Clip Art (print)
Youth Group Activities (print)
Clip Art Library Version 2.0 (CD-ROM)

Digital Resources

Clip Art Library Version 2.0 (CD-ROM)
Ideas Library on CD-ROM

Videos & Video Curricula

EdgeTV
Equipped to Serve: Volunteer Youth Worker Training Course
The Heart of Youth Ministry: A Morning with Mike Yaconelli
Good Sex: A Whole-Person Approach to Teenage Sexuality and God
Live the Life! Student Evangelism Training Kit
Purpose-Driven Youth Ministry Training Kit
Real Kids: Short Cuts
Real Kids: The Real Deal—on Friendship, Loneliness, Racism, & Suicide
Real Kids: The Real Deal—on Sexual Choices, Family Matters, & Loss
Real Kids: The Real Deal—on Stressing Out, Addictive Behavior, Great Comebacks, & Violence
Real Kids: Word on the Street
Student Underground: An Event Curriculum on the Persecuted Church
Understanding Your Teenager Video Curriculum

Student Resources

Downloading the Bible: A Rough Guide to the New Testament
Downloading the Bible: A Rough Guide to the Old Testament
Grow For It Journal
Grow For It Journal through the Scriptures
Spiritual Challenge Journal: The Next Level
Teen Devotional Bible
What Would Jesus Do? Spiritual Challenge Journal
What Almost Nobody Will Tell You About Sex
Wild Truth Journal for Junior Highers
Wild Truth Journal—Pictures of God